Work-Based Learning

The Key to School-to-Work Transition

Work-Based Learning

The Key to School-to-Work Transition

James L. Hoerner, Ph.D.
and
James B. Wehrley, Ph.D.

GLENCOE
McGraw-Hill

New York, New York   Columbus, Ohio   Woodland Hills, California   Peoria, Illinois

Library of Congress Cataloging-in-Publication Data

Hoerner, James L.
     Work-based learning : the key to school-to-work transition / James
L. Hoerner and James B. Wehrley.
          p.   cm.
     Includes bibliographical references and index.
     ISBN 0-02-801822-2
     1. Educational change—United States.   2. School-to-work
transition—United States.   I. Wehrley, James B.   II. Title.
LA217.2.H64   1994
370.973—dc20   94-35559
                                                                CIP

Work-Based Learning: The Key to School-to-Work Transition

Imprint 2000

Send all inquiries to:

Glencoe/McGraw-Hill
8787 Orion Place
Columbus, OH 43240

ISBN 0-02-801822-2

Printed in the United States of America.

5 6 7 8 9   045   02 01 00

"If you want a good economic future, there can be no simple division between work and learning."
President Bill Clinton

"Education and employment are connected and always must be."
Secretary Richard Riley, U.S. Department of Education

"We must get rid of the division between formal education and working."
Secretary Robert Reich, U.S. Department of Labor

TO ORDER ADDITIONAL COPIES OF
WORK-BASED LEARNING

Additional copies of *Work-Based Learning: The Key To School-To-Work Transition*, by Dr. James L. Hoerner and Dr. James B. Wehrley, ISBN: 0-02-801822-2, are available at a price of $15.95 each.

Please send your orders to:

Glencoe/McGraw-Hill
P.O. Box 508
Columbus, OH 43216

For further information, or to order by phone, call 1-800-334-7344.

Table of Contents

About the Authors ix

Acknowledgments xi

Preface xiii

1   Introduction 1

2   Work-Based Learning: What Is It? 9

3   The Changing Role and Philosophy of Education 16

4   Strategies for Work-Based Learning 28

5   Career Counseling and the Individual Career Development Plan 45

6   Career Majors for All—Are We Ready? 54

7   Curriculum Development for Work-Based Learning 65

8   Role of Business and Industry 83

9   Professional Development for Work-Based Learning 98

10   Steps and Strategies for Implementing Work-Based Learning 108

11   Closing Thoughts 119

Selected Readings and Bibliography 122

Index 127

About the Authors

James L. Hoerner is a professor in vocational education at Virginia Polytechnic Institute and State University. He has also been a research project director for the National Center for Research in Vocational Education, University of California, Berkeley, for the last five years. He was a dean of occupational programs at Miami Dade Community College, worked for the state department of education in California, and has seven years of trade experience as a carpenter and cabinetmaker. He is a national speaker and consultant in Tech Prep, work-based learning, school-to-work transition, and educational reform.

James B. Wehrley is an assistant professor of business administration at High Point University, High Point, North Carolina. He holds a PhD in business education from Virginia Polytechnic Institute and State University, a MBA from Baylor University, and a BBA in finance from the University of Wisconsin, Whitewater. In addition, he has five years of banking and finance experience.

Acknowledgments

It is with deep gratitude that we express our appreciation to a number of individuals without whose support this effort would not have been possible. First, we wish to express our thanks to Gray who so painstakingly devoted long hours to typing and preparing the manuscript as well as overseeing the initial editing. For her steadfast time, support, assistance, and frustrated endurance in meeting the deadlines imposed by us we are very grateful.

We also wish to acknowledge many professional colleagues and associates for their ideas, concepts, research, and publications that served as foundation and support for much of what we have written. It is, to a great extent, the development and efforts of many others that stimulated and inspired us to express our thoughts in this book.

Both of us wish to especially express our appreciation to our friends, colleagues, and scholars at Virginia Polytechnic Institute and State University and especially our associates in the Division of Vocational and Technical Education. Their professional association added encouragement and support.

To Jo Gilmore and Brian Mackin, our editors and associates at Glencoe/McGraw-Hill, we are greatly appreciative for their patience and hand-holding as we worked through the intricacies and details of the publishing process.

We want to express our sincere and grateful thanks to our families for their enduring and loving support. Jim Wehrley would like to dedicate his efforts to his parents and thank Jim Hoerner for allowing him the opportunity to participate in this endeavor.

And finally, Jim Hoerner wishes to express his deepest gratitude to Joyce Hoerner, his wife, companion, and best friend, for her patience, support, and never ending love that bring so much joy and meaning to his life.

Jim Hoerner
Jim Wehrley

Preface

We begin our discussion by raising suspicions about societies that maintain educational systems which nurture knowledge acquisition at the exclusion of knowledge application. This we believe to be the current status of the educational system in the United States, which has continued to pattern its system around a content-based process devoid of application. In fact, many in the past as well as present still look rather disdainfully on practical, applied learning that prepares one for work.

However, with many students protesting the lack of relevance in their schooling, parents questioning what they are paying for, and larger numbers of our youth not being prepared for employment, the current pattern of schooling is encountering more and more criticism. The rapid change in technology that demands increasing numbers of the work force to be academically as well as technically prepared further challenges the educational system. We also know that a highly skilled and well-educated work force is the backbone of a globally competitive nation.

As a work-oriented society that believes everyone should be an independent self-supporting productive individual, it is time to totally change the paridigm of our educational system. We must now move from a knowledge-based learning system with little connection to the real world to a work-based learning system that is positively connected to preparing everyone to be a productive contributing member of society.

Our educational system should be about preparing *everyone* to make a smooth transition from school to work. This will mean developing an educational system that is career oriented and emphasizes **work-based learning**—*the knowledge/learning imparted to every student from the beginning of schooling which maintains a theme or focus that people work to live and that there is a positive connectedness between the schooling process and living productive lives*. This is our central theme.

This book is primarily about the philosophical changes and secondarily the processes and strategies we believe are required to change the paradigm of education. We are concerned that work-based learning and other work-oriented strategies will be seen and interpreted as only an upgrade of vocational education for non-college-bound students. As you read this book, it should become increasingly clear that we are talking about changing the educational system for *all* students. We do not just address the students who typically are in the general or vocational track. One of our main points is that the ideas and concepts of work-based learning should pertain to all students. Additionally, they do not just pertain to high school and postsecondary levels. Make no mistake, we are talking about a change from kindergarten through postsecondary levels. We believe the main contribution of *Work-Based Learning* is the emphasis on systemic change for the whole schooling process. As you read this book keep that thought in mind.

James L. Hoerner
James B. Wehrley

Chapter 1

Introduction

"Societies that maintain educational systems that nurture knowledge acquisition at the exclusion of knowledge application will soon find that both their ideologies and technologies will erode."
(Hoerner, 1986)

With only 22% of the American population completing four years or more of college, we can no longer tolerate an educational system that almost exclusively emphasizes preparation for college. "[F]or every dollar in taxpayer's money invested in education of the non-college bound, fifty dollars is spent subsidizing those going to college—a ratio that is neither fair nor efficient" (Thurow, 1993, p. 275). At the same time, projections are that only one fourth of the jobs will require a bachelor's degree or above by the year 2000. As America looks toward the future, it is time to accept the premise stated by Lester Thurow in *Head to Head:* "in the twenty-first century the education and skills of a workforce will end up being the dominant competitive weapon" (1993, p. 40).

We cannot continue to perpetuate an educational system that has at least a 50% rate of failure/rejection/mismatch with its students. How many educators have thought about the rejection and mismatch that exists today for at least half of our young people? Nationally, approximately 25% of our youth drop out of high school. We also know that of the 50% of our high school graduates who start college, approximately 50% do not acquire a baccalaureate degree. Therefore, it appears that at least 50% of our young people fail, drop out, or do not complete the educational paths that they start. How many industries or businesses could stay in operation with a 50% rejection or failure rate of their products or services? This practice also results in at least 50% of our young people attempting to move into the work force with little qualification and being ill prepared for work.

Never has there been such need and opportunity to systemically change the educational system in the United States. We can no longer afford an educational system that seems less than adequate for approximately three-fourths of our youth. It is becoming increasingly obvious that, as a work-oriented society, we need an educational system with a central mission and focus to prepare *everyone* to be a productive individual and to provide a smooth transition from school to work for all students, whether they are pursuing careers as physicians, lawyers, or engineers or as nurses, computer technicians, welders, or carpenters.

This is a radical change in basic philosophy for most educators in this country, who have not been accustomed to drawing connections between the schooling process and their students' futures. In fact, one of the major dilemmas that we face is that a high percentage of the educators in America have had little experience in any environment other than education. The majority of students will need to be successful in environments other than the kind that most educators have experienced. Therefore, radical reform of the educational system and the establishment of strong connections and links with work environments outside of education will require extensive comprehensive professional development.

Work-Based Learning: The Key

As a work-oriented society, can we continue to tolerate a content-based educational system that is devoid of application and relevance for most of our youth? The time has come to systemically change from content-based learning to work-based learning if we want our students to make a smooth transition from school to work. In an educational system that has the premise "people work to live" as its central focus, all students would be encouraged to see the connection between the schooling process and their futures as productive individuals. Expressed in another way, in an educational system that is built on the work-based learning theory, all teachers would need to teach in a manner that assists their students in seeing the relevancy, application, and value to their future of what they are learning.

It is interesting to contrast 16- to 19-year-old students in America with their counterparts in selected European countries. Most would agree that a very small percentage (perhaps less than 15%) of the 16- to 19-year-olds in the United States have a fair idea of their career goals. By contrast, in Germany, Denmark, Switzerland, Sweden, Austria, and other industrialized countries, well over 70% of the 16- to 19-year-olds know their career paths and are involved in various apprenticeship programs, developing qualifications for such careers. These countries also have educational systems and national work force preparation policies to prepare everyone for productive employment. Is the United States ready to develop such a system, or are we still caught up in an elitist philosophy of *"sort out the best and forget the rest"*?

We are beginning a period of real reform and transformation of our educational system. At present the expanding wealth of literature, discussion, and research is replete with major initiatives as part of the reform efforts for the U.S. educational system. Several of the more recent work-based learning and school-to-work initiatives that are being discussed are:

1) Tech Prep,

2) integration of academic and vocational education,

3) applied academics,

4) outcome-based education,

5) apprenticeship,

6) cooperative education,

7) career academies, and

8) industry/education compacts.

At the outset, however, these initiatives will not make a major impact within the present paradigm of education. The key to the success of these initiatives rests with the classroom teachers, the practitioners interfacing with the students. Until classroom teachers recognize the need to change the basic paradigm, little change will take place.

A New Paradigm

It is now time to make a major systemic and philosophical change in the role education is to play in the twenty-first century. Currently, the major emphasis of the educational system is on content-based learning primarily for the purpose of getting students ready for college. That emphasis must shift from content-based learning to contextual, applied work-based learning. This change in emphasis will help each student relate his or her learning experience to his or her future as a productive, contributing member of society. As U.S. Assistant Secretary Kappner of the Department of Education said (1993), "we are now talking about workforce development as mainstream and center of our educational system."

The following two quotes from the National Coalition for Advanced Manufacturing (1993) position paper sums up best the need for radical change and a new paradigm for education:

> America does a brilliant job of preparing the top 20 to 25 percent of our work force, the people we rely on to invent new products and organize better processes for producing them. But when it comes to the next 75 percent of our men and women, who do not graduate from universities, and upon whose skills America's ability to produce high-productivity goods and services depends, we have fallen behind the competition.

> If we were to design a system guaranteed to produce a declining standard of living, it could not be any more brutally effective than the process we already have to prepare our people for work. . . . Unlike our competitors, the United States has **no system** [emphasis added] to assist the transition from school to the workplace or to educate and train its front-line workers (p. 5).

The necessary change implied in these two statements is a radical shift for most educators of today and requires a total systemic reform of the current system. However, to provide the educational system needed in the twenty-first century, anything short of such implied change just will not do.

As Marshall and Tucker (1992) and others have said, America has the worst school-to-work transition of any industrialized nation in the world. How much longer can we afford a "do -it-yourself" approach to the school-to-work transition process for most of our young people? Have we thought about a success-oriented educational system in which young people, after comprehensively exploring a great breadth of options, select pathways to be successful productive individuals with educators facilitating them to reach their goals?

For how many young people is the choice of going to college a choice by default, in the absence of sufficient information regarding other viable options? Are educators, in general, helping young people to know their options for being producers in life? As Boyer (1992) said in his discussion on "universality of work," every young person must be made aware that everyone, in addition to being consumers, must also be producers and that people work to live. Are educators today helping young people think through how they are going to be productive individuals, or are they just too busy disseminating knowledge?

The time has come to introduce the idea that every young person should start an Individual Career Development Plan (ICDP) initiated in the third or fourth grade. After all, we have IEPs (Individual Education Plans) for special needs students. An ICDP would serve as a means to help all young people think about their futures. Even if they change their minds many times—as they will—at least they will have a focus for their studies. Teachers could then help them relate math, science, language arts, and other subjects to such future occupations, regardless of career choice. Is there any young person today who would not benefit (including the future M.D., physicist, or engineer) from a well-thought-out ICDP that gets started in elementary school and continues through post-secondary education?

The shift in the system being suggested here is a radical change for many educators. The new paradigm would require teachers to change from content-based teaching with little application or relevancy to providing learning experiences that are grounded in the concept that everyone must be a productive member of society. This shift to work-based learning—learning oriented toward being a worker someday—could be the single greatest change that needs to be made in our current educational system.

Questions Needing Answers

Someone once said that change does not happen until we start to ask ourselves some of the right questions. It is time for educators at all levels to rethink several important questions. How many classroom teachers have had the opportunity, as part of a professional development day, to debate the question:

- What is the purpose of the educational system today and in the future?

Have the administrators in our elementary and secondary schools and community colleges—or, for that matter, even our colleges and universities—organized such discussions? Several other questions that should also be debated include the following:

- In a work-oriented society, what is the role of the educational system in preparing the work force?
- Who should provide the education needed for individuals to be successful in the workplace?
- Who should provide the education for careers that require B.S., M.S., Ph.D., and M.D. degrees for engineers, scientists, school teachers, medical doctors, and the like?

We know the answer to this last question. None of us complain about supporting, through taxes, the greatest higher educational system in the world to prepare the top 20–30% of the work force.

The question that now needs to be answered is:

- Who should provide the education for the 70% of the work force who do not need a bachelor's degree or more?

That's the question work-based learning strategies such as Tech Prep, apprenticeship, career academies, co-op, and other school-to-work initiatives are addressing. It is interesting that no one expresses concern about supporting an educational system or public schooling process to prepare physicians, lawyers, engineers, and scientists through reasonably costly professional schools that are, we hope, very work oriented. Yet many people express concern about including work-oriented programs to prepare machinists, welders, computer technicians, carpenters, aviation mechanics, and the like in the schooling process in this country. It is also interesting to note that the levels of science and mathematics required to perform in many of the non-university-driven careers are just as high as, if not higher than, those required in many of the university-driven careers.

These questions must be discussed by all classroom teachers, counselors, and administrators as we look toward reforming and restructuring our educational system. Are the administrators, principals, superintendents, deans, presidents, and university professors providing classroom teachers with the opportunities to rethink and reexamine the purpose of education today as we move into the twenty-first century?

As was stated earlier, "Societies that maintain educational systems that nurture knowledge acquisition at the exclusion of knowledge application will soon find that both their ideologies and technologies will erode" (Hoerner, 1986). Is this still the problem of the educational system in this country? The United States, of course, adopted the British educational system that practiced the elitist separation of knowing and doing. One of the major problems in America's educational system is that we continue to perpetuate a system that keeps *learning for knowing* separate from *learning for doing*. Where did the idea of teaching content devoid of application or relevance come from? No doubt, the first form of teaching in the history of humankind must have been very applications-oriented as Neanderthals taught their children to point a stick to spear fish in the nearby river.

It is important that we now greatly change the system—perhaps rethink the system and develop a new paradigm for education. Work-based learning has the potential to be the new paradigm and bring together *learning for knowing* and for *doing* for all of our young people—especially the forgotten majority.

A New Mission

The new mission for education is found in goal 3, Title I of "Goals 2000: Educate America Act," which states, "By the year 2000 . . . every school in America will ensure that all students . . . be prepared for responsible citizenship, further learning, and productive employment in our modern economy" (103rd Congress, 1st session, 1993, p. 3). We need to rethink a new vision for education (Fiske, 1991, *Smart Schools, Smart Kids*). It is now time for a new mission in education in America. On the PBS-TV program "Keeping America Number One," which was broadcast on July 31, 1992, it was said, "we need an educational system that supports what is needed to lead productive lives." Also, the Council of Chief State School Officers (CCSSO) stated in their 1991 policy statement, "schools must view preparation of youth for employment as part of their primary responsibility" (CCSSO, 1991, p. 7).

The time has come for *all* educational institutions to adopt the mission to prepare *all* students for (1) further learning, (2) citizenship, and (3) productive employment. Since we are a work-oriented society and belive in lifelong learning, is there any young person today who does not need to be prepared for all three? As was already mentioned, we have an educational system that is preparing the top 20–30% for further learning and productive employment. After all, further learning is the purpose of attending a four-year college or university. However, even if you pursue a liberal arts degree, you are expected to get further preparation to be employable through:

1) graduate work,
2) employment by a business or industry that will provide the education and training to be productive, or
3) going back to a community college to learn employable skills.

That is why a significant number of the new students in our 1250-plus community and technical colleges in the United States already have bachelor's degrees. According to the American Association for Community Colleges, as many as 30% of the new students in many of our community and technical colleges have at least a bachelor's degree.

So what is being suggested is that we develop an educational system that sees its responsibility to prepare *everyone* for *further learning* and *productive employment*. That is the focus of applied work-based learning; and, if done correctly, work-based learning can be the pathway to provide the same educational opportunity to the 70% who do not need a bachelor's degree as is provided to those pursuing the baccalaureate. Most classroom teachers and, for that matter, most educators still do not believe that their job includes preparing everyone for productive employment. Of course, we now ask: Are the universities who are the "makers of educators" currently preparing teachers, counselors, and administrators to respond to the new mission?

Summary

The time has come to make major, systemic change in the role our educational system plays in today's society. We must shift from a knowledge, content-based educational system to a system in which the major purpose is to develop success-oriented pathways of learning through which everyone is being prepared to be an independent, self-supporting, productive, and contributing member of society, regardless of one's career direction. This will necessitate that all educators shift from being disseminators of knowledge to facilitators of learning for life's applications. Our educational institutions must adopt the mission to prepare *every* student for further learning and productive employment, whether he or she is going to be a lawyer, medical doctor, bulldozer driver, nurse, computer operator, or aviation mechanic.

We are not advocating an educational system that emphasizes job preparation at the expense of academic preparation and the arts and humanities. To be a productive citizen in today's society, everyone needs a balanced mix of academic and technical preparation. We also know that producing educated individuals who cannot get jobs does not help the individual or society. It has been said that it's hard to appreciate poetry on an empty stomach. As Secretary Reich suggested in the September 22, 1993, National Center for Research in Vocational Education teleconference, we must get rid of the division between formal education and working.

It is now time for educators at all levels to rethink the process called education and listen to the studies about the role of education in today's society. Then we must set out to change what we are doing to what we need to do. If we want a success-oriented school-to-work transition for *all* of our students, we must have an educational system that provides applied work-based learning for *all* and terminate the elitist philosophy of "career-bound" versus "college-bound" students.

To change the paradigm for education to what it must become as we go toward the twenty-first century, the following two basic reform shifts must take place:

- *All educators* must recognize that preparing *all* students to be successful, productive individuals needs to become a central focus for the educational system of America.
- All students must experience the CONNECTION and relationship between the schooling process and their future success as productive individuals in society.

Work-based learning is the key for the new educational paradigm that can provide effective school-to-work transition for all students to be productive, contributing members of society.

References

Boyer, E.L. (1992, November). "Curriculum, Culture and Social Cohesion." *Leadership Abstracts* 5(2). Laguna, CA: League for Innovation in the Community College.

Council of Chief State School Officers. (1991). *Connecting School and Employment*. Policy Statement L99-1. Washington, D.C.

Fiske, E.B. (1991). *Smart Schools, Smart Kids*. New York: Simon & Schuster.

Hoerner, J.L. (1986). "Another Look at the Philosophy of Education." A lecture given at Wolverhampton Polytechnic, Wolverhampton, England.

Kappner, A. (1993, January). A speech given at the League for Innovation in the Community College Workforce 2000 Conference. New Orleans, LA.

Marshall, R. & Tucker, M. (1992). *Thinking for a Living: Education and the Wealth of Nations*. New York: Basic Books, Harper Collins.

National Coalition for Advanced Manufacturing. (1993). "Preparing Technical Workers for the New Industrial Era: The Need for a Fundamental Shift in Federal Policy Toward Technical Education." A position paper. Washington, D.C.

103rd Congress, 1st Session (1993, October 18). Goals 2000: Educate America Act. H.R. 1804 in the Senate of the United States.

Reich, R. & Riley, R. (1993, September). "Breaking the Mold." National Center for Research in Vocational Education teleconference.

Thurow, L.C. (1993). *Head to Head*. New York: Warner Books.

Chapter **2**

Work-Based Learning: What Is It?

"The lack of any clear, direct connection between education and employment opportunities for most young people is one of the most devastating aspects of the existing system."
(Commission on the Skills of the American Workforce, 1990)

In Chapter 1 we presented an introduction and overview of several concepts that are discussed further in this and later chapters. The basic premise established in Chapter 1 was that radical change is needed in the current educational system, which implies radical philosophical change in the schooling process. However, we have saved our discussion on philosophy for Chapter 3 so that we can first address work-based learning.

Until recently, education that dealt with work occurred primarily within the confines of vocational education. Since the late 1800s, many publications have been written about the relationship of education and work. Much of the past discussion has focused on the value of vocational education as a contributing component to public education. In his book *Education and Work for the Year 2000: Choices We Face*, A. G. Wirth (1992) provided a superb overview of the historical development of vocational education; we will therefore not retrace such development in this discussion.

In the 1990s, interest in work-based learning has continued to expand. The passing of the Carl D. Perkins Vocational and Applied Technology Education Act on September 25, 1990, with the inclusion of the Tech Prep Education Act, brought forth an increased emphasis on school-to-work programs and work-based learning initiatives. Since the Tech Prep Act, a national movement has taken place to expand relevant programs of learning for a greater number of young people. The Tech Prep initiative strongly encourages applied, contextual learning. As a result, much greater emphasis has been put on developing programs that have connection to employment and contribute to a smoother school-to-work transition.

Simon, Dippo, and Schenke (1991) in their book *Learning Work: A Critical Pedagogy of Work Education* defined work education as a practice that emphasizes the development of knowledge, skills, and attitudes that relate to a student's future participation within the economic sector of one's community and nation. In practice, such intentions became manifest in a considerable variety of program forms including career exploration, world of work, adult retraining, work transition, and high school and college work-study courses that combine alternating periods of time in schools and workplaces (p. ix).

With the increased interest in reforming the American educational system and the need to make the system more relevant for a larger number of students, there has been more discussion recently about school-to-work and work-based programs being for *all* students. On the "Breaking the Mold" national teleconference sponsored by the National Center for Research in Vocational Education, Secretaries of Labor and Education Reich and Riley both discussed the need for all students to have work-based experiences that parallel their school-based learning.

The recently passed School-to-Work Opportunities Act of 1994 includes in Section 101, General Program Requirements, that all students will have access to both school-based and work-based components. This new act has evoked a magnitude of discussion about work-based learning and the hands-on experiences that today's youth should receive as part of the schooling process. While the term "work-based learning" is used numerous times in the new act, it does not specifically define work-based learning. Section 103, Work-Based Learning Component, lists five components for work-based learning: (1) work experience, (2) a planned program of job training and work experience, (3) workplace mentoring, (4) instruction in general workplace competencies, and (5) broad instruction in a variety of elements of an industry (103 Congress, May 1994). The School-to-Work Opportunities Act also discusses the importance of the linkage of the school-based and work-based activities.

We believe that the key to school-to-work transition for most young people greatly depends on the success of the work-based learning component as part of the schooling process. Therefore, the way in which educators view the concept of work-based learning is important. We believe that there are two definitions for work-based learning and that each is very important.

Definition One for Work-Based Learning

The first definition is more traditional and aligns with the new School-to-Work Opportunities Act.

> **Work-Based Learning:**   Learning experiences and activities that are based *on* and *in* some type of work setting or simulated work setting, that is, apprenticeship, internship, co-op, on-the-job training, career academies, school-based enterprises, occupational/technical labs, job simulation, and the like.

This form of work-based learning includes job-based experiences as well as contrived and simulated work activities duplicating the work setting. While some have expressed that work-based learning experiences need to be job-based to provide the most appropriate experience, it must be recognized that, owing to a number of factors, it will be virtually impossible to provide for a large quantity of students. It has become evident that few employers are able to provide meaningful work-based learning experiences for a large number of students that allow students to apply high-level academic and occupational knowledge. *America's Choice* and other studies have shown that the majority of workplaces are still operating according to the old style of work organization in which workers perform tasks over and over, and therefore, many workplaces are unable to offer meaningful work-based learning experiences. Also, geographic location can play a role in the availability of job-based experiences; for example, in rural America, not every school is located where it is logistically possible to provide a variety of job-based experiences. Additionally, because of economic conditions, certain work experiences might not always be available.

Educators should not use such situations and conditions as reasons for not providing appropriate hands-on experiences. Instead, creative alternative strategies must be developed and employed. When various conditions preclude real job experiences, then a variety of school-based work experiences and activities should be developed as well as joint initiatives involving schools and community-based organizations. The following are lists of work-based learning activities that can provide hands-on experiences:

I. School-Based Work Experiences

1) school-based enterprises
2) career academies
3) customer service labs
4) job shop labs
5) job simulation labs
6) vocational/occupational labs
7) mock business/industry projects
8) senior and class projects

II. Job-Based Work Experiences

1) apprenticeship
2) cooperative education
3) clinical
4) on-the-job training (OJT)
5) mentorship
6) internship
7) aligned work-study programs
8) school-linked summer employment
9) community service learning
10) business/education compacts

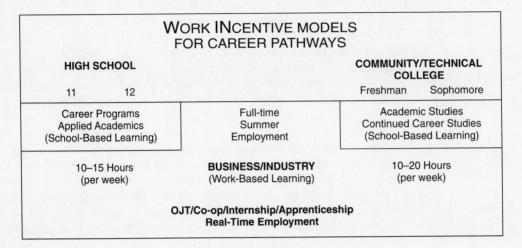

Figure 2.1
WIN Model for Career Pathways

While the above lists are not intended to be inclusive, the important point is that educators, with the assistance of business and industry partnerships, need to develop a wide variety of work-based, job-related, hands-on experiences for all students. The WIN Model for Career Pathways (Figure 2.1) is a scheme that provides work-based learning experiences that parallel school-based activities (Hoerner, 1994, p. 10). Such a model for *all* students would greatly enhance the school-to-work transition process. Is there any student, including the future scientist, physician, engineer, nurse, computer technician, or carpenter, who would not benefit from a work-based experience that parallels the school-based activities?

Definition Two for Work-Based Learning

As was previously mentioned, we believe that there is a second definition for work-based learning. The second definition, while less obvious, is of even greater importance than the first. When we speak of *Work-Based Learning: The Key to School-to-Work Transition*, we believe that the key rests mostly with the second definition as a broader way of looking at work-based learning. Until all educators throughout the schooling/learning process recognize that there must now be a positive connection for *all* students between education and living productive lives, we will continue to perpetuate the academic versus the vocational mentality.

Work-Based Learning: The knowledge/learning imparted to every student from the beginning of schooling that maintains a theme or focus that people work to live and that there is a positive connectedness between the schooling process and living productive lives.

This second definition is absent from our schools and needs to be developed extensively throughout the schooling/learning process. As Boyer (1992) indicated, children grow up not knowing that people work to live and that young people must understand the processes of production and consumption. He further suggested that students study culture through the prism of work: Who works?, What work is prized?, and so on.

This second definition of work-based learning relates content areas from elementary school through college to an individual's future. It insists on a purpose and reason for learning. This method of teaching/learning often provokes much controversy, especially among academic educators who are discipline- or content-oriented and do not know work applications for the content they are expecting their students to learn.

We view this second definition of work-based learning as the key to change and reform that must take place in the schooling process. With the use of work-based learning techniques, young people in elementary school can begin to see the connections between their schooling experiences and what adults do to make a living. They will begin to see the reasons for learning and what is expected of them. Young people will also begin to recognize the value and benefits of work and not view it as drudgery or a necessary evil, as is too often the case. This view is especially likely if being a productive, contributing member of society is ignored or is not discussed in a positive sense. It is valid to help all young people recognize that, as someone once said, "Work is our key source for wealth." Are all educators at all levels helping young people see that, through employment and working, one can have those objects and characteristics that are most valued: a feeling of self-worth and confidence, a good standard of living, and the resources to do what they want and have the possessions and experiences they want? Educators, through drawing the connections between school and work, have the opportunity to help our youth value being good workers, good team members, and contributing members of society. Elementary teachers can start young people thinking about how they are going to make their living by discussing the connections between what is being studied in class and how it can be applied so that the student becomes a valued worker in the future. Second and third graders can discuss and think about what their parents, family members, and neighbors do and how they might use the math, science, and language arts concepts being discussed when they are workers in the community—and how such work translates into the clothes, food, and home they have.

Arts and humanities teachers, in addition to teaching subjects that enrich lives, can draw connections between what is being studied and the student's future as a member of the work force and the community. From discussions with many young as well as older students, it is apparent that teachers at most levels of education frequently fail to help students grasp application and relevance. For this reason, many young people are asking why they need such knowledge. While many educators of today will not agree, if a teacher in any subject or discipline cannot give valid reasons for learning something beyond "because I say so" or "so you can go to college," one wonders why the subject should be learned. Too often, young people do not see the connection between what they are doing in school and how they plan to put a roof over their head, food in their mouth, and clothes on their back as a self-supporting, independent, and contributing member of society. Again, being a good worker is the main source of these elements for most of society. Are educators providing this focus? This mode of learning based on someday being a good worker provides a focus for young people in the early grades (second, third, and fourth grades) so that they can relate what they are learning to future applications that have value for them. Instead of just learning textbook material or what the teacher dictates, perhaps students may then begin to develop a desire to acquire knowledge that they know they will need to fulfill future needs and desires.

If these connections being discussed are commonplace at the elementary levels, students will expect that later educational experiences will also have relevance to their futures. High school and postsecondary learning, including college and university experiences, will need to have relevance also. Educators, including those at the university level, are not accustomed to drawing these linkages.

Summary

As policy makers, educators, business/industry leaders, and society at large recognize that the current antiquated model is no longer appropriate for our schooling process, developing greater connections between education and work is increasingly important. We must move to work-based learning—learning that is *based on* working and being productive. We have too long perpetuated an educational system that has demonstrated little inclination to be relevant to students' futures. In fact, the educational system of this country has often prided itself on its climate of elitism and being above the practical. This time has passed. To produce "educated" individuals who cannot get jobs because of a schooling process that has little relevance to one's ability to make a living, is becoming increasingly unsatisfactory. Again, as a society we need to ask ourselves why we have an educational system. What is the purpose of the schooling process if it is not to help individuals live successful lives along with being good community citizens? In a work-oriented society, everyone needs to work to make a living. To compete globally in the future world economy, the United States must have a well-educated work force.

Greater connections between school and work must now be developed. For too long, too many young people have been experiencing too little relevance in the schooling process. This school experience continues to result in low achievement. The key rests with the way in which we teach or present what is expected to be achieved. The expected level of achievement is not out of reach for most young people. The critical point is that material be presented in an applied manner and that the learner see the relevance and connection to future applications.

The key then rests with a schooling process that constantly helps students to see the relevance in what they are learning and connections to their future as well as hands-on, applied learning throughout the schooling process. Recent studies reflect that we need radical change not only at the elementary and secondary levels, but also at the postsecondary, college, and university levels.

Therefore, it is now time to radically change the system and build greater connections between all levels of the schooling process and being productive individuals. That is what the concepts of work-based learning represent.

All students at all levels deserve to know the connections between the schooling process and their future lives as self-supporting, contributing members of society.

References

Boyer, E.L. (1992, November). "Curriculum, Culture and Social Cohesion." *Leadership Abstracts 5*(2). Laguna, CA: League for Innovation in the Community College.

Commission on the Skills of the American Workforce. (1990). *America's Choice: High Skills or Low Wages*. Rochester, NY.

Hoerner, J.L. (1994, February-March). "Work-Based Learning: The Key to School-to-Work Transition." *ATEA Journal 21*(3), pp. 6–10.

101st Congress (1990, September). Carl D. Perkins Vocational and Applied Technology Education Act Amendments of 1990.

103rd Congress (1994, May). School-to-Work Opportunities Act of 1994.

Simon, R., Dippo, D. & Schenke, A. (1991). *Learning Work: A Critical Pedagogy of Work Education*. New York: Bergin & Garvey.

Wirth, A. G. (1992). *Education and Work for the Year 2000: Choices We Face*. San Francisco: Jossey-Bass.

Chapter **3**

The Changing Role and Philosophy of Education

"One overriding question—are young people learning what they need to learn to compete and win in a global economy?"
(President Clinton at American Council on Education Meeting, 1994)

President Clinton posed the question cited here because he is challenging society at large, and educators specifically, to truly examine how well our present educational system is preparing young people for their futures. The United States has faced this dilemma since at least 1983 when the National Commission on Excellence in Education study, *A Nation at Risk: The Imperative for Educational Reform,* was released. Since then there have been additional studies encouraging educational reform; however, little change has occurred. We should ask ourselves—*why*

Although we don't have any easy answers, in this chapter we speculate on several of the problems and the changes that need to be made. In Chapters 1 and 2 we alluded to the importance of change and systemic reform of the total educational system. We also discussed how we believe the answer will be found in a system built around the two definitions of work-based learning presented in Chapter 2. The primary conceptual change we believe must take place, however, is embedded in definition two, which emphasizes a prevailing theme or focus throughout the educational system that people must work to live and that there is a "connectedness" between the schooling process and living productive lives. This, of course, necessitates radical change in the basic foundations and philosophies of the current educational system. To recommend a strong connection between the schooling process and being a productive citizen when the educational system has generally been disconnected from work suggests the current system is outdated.

Evidence for Change

Before discussing the changes needed in the system, we first present a number of facts and ideas that support the need for change. The following findings of the School-to-Work Opportunities Act of 1994 support that change is needed (103rd Congress, 1994, sec. 2, pp. 4–5):

- ■ ". . . Three fourths of the high school students in the United States enter the workforce without baccalaureate degrees, and many do not possess the academic and entry-level occupational skills necessary to succeed in the changing United States workplace. . . ."

- ■ ". . . A substantial number of youths in the United States, especially disadvantaged students . . . and students with disabilities, do not complete high school. . . ."

- ■ ". . . Unemployment among youths in the United States is intolerably high, . . ."

- ■ ". . . The workplace in the United States is changing in response to heightened international competition and new technologies, and such forces, which are ultimately beneficial to the nation, are shrinking the demand for and undermining the earning power of unskilled labor. . . ."

- ■ ". . . The United States lacks a comprehensive and coherent system to help youths acquire the knowledge, skills, abilities, and information about and access to the labor market necessary to make an effective transition from school to career-oriented work or to further education. . . ."

- ■ ". . . There is infrequent linkage between . . . jobs and . . . the career planning or exploration, or the school-based learning of students. . . ."

- ■ ". . . Work-based learning . . . integrates theoretical instruction with structured on-the-job training, and this approach, combined with school-based learning, can be very effective in engaging student interest, enhancing skill acquisition, developing positive work attitudes, and preparing youths for high-skill, high-wage careers. . . ."

There is no end to the evidence that relates and supports the need for greater linkage between school and work. All one needs to do is talk to workers at most levels and ask them how much their schooling experiences prepared them for work; most will reflect and answer that there was little connection. The recent Gallup survey reported by Lester (1994) at the National Press Club in Washington, D.C., revealed astounding figures: Almost two thirds of the adults in the United States think public high schools are not devoting enough attention to helping non-college-bound students develop the skills they need to find jobs after they graduate. Seventy-two percent of the adults indicated that if they could repeat their education, they would want more information about future careers (Lester, 1994).

Furthermore, a large number of high school students in the United States see little connection or relevance between their schooling experiences and their futures. This absence of relevance results in boredom and, in turn, unmotivated students who will do only enough to "get by and get out."

Growing evidence also indicates that public colleges and universities are not doing an outstanding job at providing career development. A spring 1993 survey of students at 36 colleges and universities revealed that the top four educational and personal areas of need were related to career development. According to Muffo (1994), the four areas in order of highest need from a list of 59 were the following:

- obtaining work experience in career areas
- learning about job opportunities
- developing effective job-seeking skills
- arranging to discuss career interests with people employed in area of career choice.

The survey is the standardized College Needs Assessment Survey administered to randomly selected samples of 1000 undergraduates at each of the participating universities. The results of the survey revealed that approximately two thirds of the college and university undergraduates need help with career development. It is important to note that figures also indicate seniors feel they need just as much assistance with career development as freshmen. When the figures were shared with various university department faculty, the general response was that career development is not the role of universities. Increasingly larger numbers of college and university graduates are not employable without further education and preparation either through graduate work, business/industry training, or occupational preparation at a community or technical college. These findings only further support the antiquated philosophies that still permeate the ivory towers of academe that have little inclination to relate to the real world and the futures of their students.

Muffo also reported from the Pew Higher Education Roundtable that, "Parents now ask institutions [of higher education] with growing bluntness, 'What exactly are we paying for?' and they measure the quality of higher education in terms of their children's ability to garner secure and well-paying jobs" (p. 1).

When one listens to industry representatives about what they want in a new employee and then assess what is being taught in our schools, the mismatch is clear. At a February 1994 education conference in Florida, five industry speakers addressed 200 secondary educators. Their topic addressed the qualifications industry is looking for in new employees. There was consensus that the nondegreed graduate employee needed the following characteristics or skills:

1) good attitude
2) commitment
3) basic technical skill
4) basic communication/writing and math skills
5) adaptable and flexible
6) dependable
7) open to further learning
8) customer service skills
9) punctual
10) at work every day

11) teamwork skills

12) problem-solving skills

13) computer skills

14) leadership skills

15) some work experience

The 200 educators present were asked to seriously assess their 17- to 19-year-old students in each of these 15 categories. When asked how many felt 100% of their students, 17 to 19, possessed all 15 characteristics sufficiently adequate to meet industry needs, no hands were raised. No hands were raised indicating 75% or 50% of the high school students had such skills. Finally, after further questioning, approximately a third of the 200 educators indicated that 25–30% of their high school graduates probably had sufficient skills in the 15 areas to be employed. Having conducted this same informal survey with a cumulative total of approximately 2000 secondary educators in at least 10 other states, the responses were similar. While only an informal survey, these results are no doubt reasonably representative of how teachers would respond in the majority of schools throughout the country. It is rather disturbing that the majority of our secondary students are graduating from high school without the basic employability skills that business and industry desire (as assessed by their own teachers). Again, it is appropriate to ask: What is the purpose of our schools if it is not to prepare our young people for their futures?

We could present many examples and supporting evidence that preparing young people for employment is not the central goal of the schooling process. Changes in the basic paradigm of the current system must take place. Until the basic underlying premise of education is shifted from content-based learning, devoid of application, to work-based learning that prepares people for productive employment, little change will result.

The Traditional System: A Brief Review

Before discussing the changes needed in the educational system let's review how the current educational system appears to have evolved. Most of us would speculate that the earliest teaching and learning in the history of humankind was very application oriented. Again, we ask: Where did the concept of teaching content, devoid of application or relevancy, come from? The current educational structure seems to have emerged primarily from Plato and the ancient Greek academic system. Plato and his Academy, according to Clinchy (1994), created the original groves of academe by establishing the first real "campus" away from the business and political life of the marketplace. The Academy, set off by itself, was devoted to cultivating the mind and educating a select elite group of young people, relatively free from the distractions of the workaday world. This early pattern that our present schooling process models was established for the elite, not for the commoner who needed to learn applied, work-oriented skills.

Schools have traditionally been intellectually and educationally isolated from the everyday life of their students and the larger society (Clinchy, 1994).

The separation and "disconnection" between the life of the mind and the ordinary, everyday life of the nonacademic society started in the classical civilizations of Greece and Rome. In both the ancient world and the Middle Ages the disconnection from the "real world" was embodied first in the fact that admission to the early universities and monasteries was limited to a select few. The vast majority of the populace and the everyday world in which they lived was studiously shunned. This disconnection was further reinforced by a curriculum that consisted of the study of grammar, rhetoric, logic, and liberal arts. The learned elite of the time found themselves most often dealing, not with everyday reality, but with painfully abstruse topics, many of them having to do with language itself and with recondite theological issues of God and the logic of a Trinity. The separation and disconnection was even further sealed and made irrevocable by the simple fact that early university and monastery-based learning was conducted and written in Latin, a language the common people of the day could not understand and to which they had no access.

This elitist attitude of the "educated" and "learned" academics of the colleges and universities has continued since medieval times to exert a pervasive control through a highly academic, disconnected system of lower education for all young people. Both the disconnected intellectual content of the formal academic curriculum and the disconnected instructional model created in our elementary and secondary schools were the brainchildren of the disciplinary elitists in the world of higher education. Early in this century the strictly academic curriculum and the practices of scholarly instruction were wedded to the disconnected and thoroughly mechanical practices of the scientific engineers of the industrial management movement. This marriage brought forth the "Great American Academic and Social Sorting Factory School System" that we still struggle with today (Clinchy, 1994).

Today's model of education is very much based on competition, which begins in kindergarten and culminates in the final academic cleansing by the college admissions tests. Such exams for many young people end the scholastic sorting and elimination process that attempts to fix young people's places in life by excluding them from higher education.

As Clinchy stated, this "intellectual oligarchy" will endure as long as our colleges and universities continue to use the results of standardized paper-and-pencil tests of academic skill and high school grades in the conventional subjects as determinants of access to higher education and its social and economic rewards. Our institutions of higher education are thus able to keep all of our lower schools in thrall to their "disconnected," "decontextualized" educational mission.

As we have stated, the U.S. educational system seems to be caught up in "sort out the best and forget the rest." The content requirements for learning are dictated by college and university admissions standards with little, if any, consideration given to the required levels of knowledge needed to practice various careers.

An example of the sorting process is the way the current system uses mathematics. There appears to be little evidence that most of the jobs or careers demanding a bachelor's degree or above require a high level of mathematics to practice in those careers. Yet to get the opportunity to pursue such jobs or careers, three to four years of math are required at the high school level with at least another course or two of mathematics required at the college level. Very few of us know many businesspersons, physicians, attorneys, or schoolteachers, for example, who use algebra, trigonometry, or calculus on a regular basis. In fact, it has been stated that 95% of the jobs in the United States do not require algebra to perform them satisfactorily. Yet no major studies have challenged the rationale for the mathematics requirements at either the high school or college levels. It would be very interesting research to determine the level of mathematics needed to be successful in many of the baccalaureate-driven careers. Many careers not requiring university degrees have a substantially higher mathematics requirement for successful practice than do many of the university-driven careers. Careers including carpentry, machining, sheet metal working, cabinetmaking, and other trade areas all require higher math to successfully perform on a daily basis than do the university-driven careers such as medicine, law, and business.

So, as Clinchy (1994) stated, we remain trapped in the "Great American Academic and Social Sorting Factory School System" that still believes it is necessary to sort out who will join the elite. Can we afford to tolerate and perpetuate an educational system that seems to be so decontextualized and disconnected from real life in the real world? The basic disconnected foundation, antiquated philosophy, and mission that still permeate the current schooling process needs to be challenged and reexamined. Policy makers, educators, community leaders, and society at large must be held accountable and asked to rethink: What is the purpose of the schooling process as we approach the twenty-first century?

Changing the Basic Paradigm—Can We Do It?

The United States has a unique window of opportunity to systemically reform its educational system. With the recent passage of the "Goals 2000: Educate America Act" (March 1994) and the "School-to-Work Opportunities Act of 1994" (May 1994), there is increasing momentum and support to radically change our educational structure. These two landmark acts, along with growing momentum from research studies, business and industry support, and society's discontented feelings about schools, are resulting in a major thrust to change the basic paradigm of the educational system. The need for a stronger connection between the schooling process and being prepared for employment in this work-oriented society is becoming evident.

Many studies conducted during the past several years have shown that we must greatly change the schooling process in America to bring greater relevancy into the classroom and to promote linkages between schooling and employment. The major question seems to be focused primarily on the linkage between the school curriculum and employment. Simon, Dippo, and Schenko (1991) have suggested that such linkage is of major concern to youth, parents, teachers, businesses, labor organizations, and government. Wirth (1992), in his book *Education and Work for the Year 2000: Choices We Face*, discussed at length the need for growing connections between schooling and employment. He noted, as have others, that approximately 20% of the jobs require university preparation, which matches the percentage of America's young preparing for such jobs. For the other 80% however, the picture is very different. There is the growing dualism in the quality of education received by the upper 20% and the remaining 80%. Our educational system must provide an education in work skills as well as academic experiences for the 80% which assures that they, too, are prepared for the modern work force in the global economy. We are currently devoting $55 of taxpayers' money to support the university-bound student for every dollar spent on the non-university-bound student (Thurow, 1993). To continue to invest large amounts of support and effort for the 20% or more who attend universities and ignore the other 80% is no longer acceptable. As Wirth (1992) said, to create a society with schools that prepare everyone for a world class economy will demand a dramatic change in priorities. As a result, the highest priority for every educator should be to radically change the whole basic paradigm and philosophical purpose of our educational system. The paradigm for education must now shift from a content-oriented educational system, devoid of application, to a success-oriented schooling process that prepares everyone to be self-support- ing, productive individuals. This is a radical philosophical shift for most educators who have not felt the need to draw connections between what they do in the schooling process and the applications of that process to their students' futures. To change the basic paradigm and purpose of the current educational system requires that educators at all levels make several mind-set changes relating to the role of education in society.

First, educators must stop practicing education as if there are two worlds. Willard Wirtz stated, "There aren't two worlds—*Education* and *Work*. There is one world—*LIFE*. Learning by hands-on participation . . . should be at the heart of our education perspective" (William T. Grant Foundation Commission on Work, Family and Citizenship, 1988, p. 3). Educators have kept alive the myth that *this is education; later on, someplace else, is the world of work.* We need to build partnerships and linkages with business and industry wherever possible. The Council of Chief State School Officers included as their 1991 Policy State- ment: "Connecting school and employment" (p. 1). Are all classroom teachers thinking this way yet? Work-based learning is about bringing education and work into one world.

A second basic change deals with the way educators view their role in human resource development. Human resource development has been viewed as a corporate term. Yet what are educators doing if it is not *human resource development?* They do not manufacture widgets or gadgets. They don't service automobiles or tractors. They are developing human resources.

Many studies have discussed the role of education in developing the work force. In their book *Building a Quality Workforce*, McLaughlin, Bennett, and Verity (1988) said, "Education has the primary responsibility for initially preparing the entry level workforce" (p. 2). Note they did not say the primary responsibility for initially preparing only the top 20–30% of the work force. The document *America's Choice: High Skills or Low Wages* states, "Guaranteeing the right to a good education to every young American and providing positive links between educational achievement and jobs are essential to the creation of an educated nation" (Commission on Skills of the American Workforce, 1990, p. 72). Fiske (1991) in *Smart Schools: Smart Kids* commented, "The consequences of becoming a learning society are enormous, for it means that for the first time schools have been given the job of producing the 'capital' on which the country depends" (p. 23). Do all classroom teachers, counselors, and administrators in our educational system today believe this? We will not truly reform education to be in the business of serving all our youth until educators accept this concept.

And yet we continue to ignore these studies. These are true indicators that support the major role educators, at all levels, must play in preparing the work force. They all agree we need to rethink how educators view their role. To see educators' role as human resource developers instead of disseminators of knowledge is a major paradigm shift for the total system. We would approach our clients, the students, differently if we accepted our role as human resource developers. This, in fact, may be the single biggest shift that is necessary to form the new paradigm for education. Work-based learning is the business of human resource development.

Someone once said that students learn best in schools that have a theme like aviation schools, business schools, and cosmetology schools. Educators should consider putting a new sign on their schools that says A Human Resource Development Institute. What a positive message that would convey to the students and community.

A third change educators must make is to stop perpetuating an educational system that advocates everyone pursue a bachelor's degree. It is now accepted that more than 70% of the jobs in America will not require a four-year college education by the year 2000. Yet educators continue to perpetuate a system that places most of its emphasis on the four-year college bound. As Hilary Pennington (1992), president of Jobs For the Future, stated, "We continue to behave as if college is the only route to success." This emphasis on university degrees could, to a certain extent, be the fault of educators, since most traveled the university route and are not very well acquainted with nonuniversity career pathways.

A fourth philosophical change is to eliminate the dual-purpose system of preparing for work or for college. How many of today's educators continue to ask their students, "Are you going to work or to college"? We must terminate such dual tracking as vocational or academic; tech prep or college prep; career bound or college bound. These terms imply an elitist mentality that only serves to perpetuate the "white collar" versus "blue collar" mind-set and the class system of the haves and have-nots. It is time to develop an educational system that impartially prepares *all* persons for productive lives regardless of their career directions.

From Content-Based to Work-Based Learning

Our educational system needs to initiate applied work-based learning strategies throughout the schooling process. When thinking of the shift from content-based education to applied work-based education, I'm reminded of how I taught high school algebra at Pioneer High School in San Jose, California, in 1963. That is right, that is what I did—I taught high school algebra. I did not teach kids. I taught algebra. An interesting exercise is to walk through the halls of educational institutions, including universities and community colleges, and ask people what they teach. They will say math, science, electronics, engineering, agriculture, home economics, and so on. No one will say kids, students, or people. That is a mind-set. Perhaps our major role as educators needs to change from disseminators of knowledge and content merchants to human resource developers and people growers (Hoerner, 1994).

To further answer the question "Why applied work-based learning?" perhaps the old Chinese proverb tells us best: I hear and I forget; I see and I remember; I do and I understand. The learning theorists and cognitive scientists also suggest that we learn 10% through hearing, 15% through seeing, 40% through seeing and hearing, and 80% by experiencing and doing. That is, we only comprehend 10% if audio is the sole medium, whereas we comprehend 80% when we experience and perform an action. There is further support for shifting to applied work-based curriculum for learning. *America's Choice* states, "The lack of any clear, direct connection between education and employment opportunities for most young people is one of the most devastating aspects of the existing system" (Commission on the Skills of the American Workforce, 1990, p. 72). The *SCANS Report: What Work Requires of Schools* supports work-based learning strategies in this statement: "All young Americans should leave school with the know-how they need to make their way in the world" (Secretary's Commission on Achieving Necessary Skills, 1991, p. vi).

Lynn Martin, former Secretary of Labor, called it *contextual learning* and said schools must teach with work in mind. The most effective way of learning is in context, placing learning objectives within a real environment rather than insisting that students learn first in the abstract what they will be expected to apply (Secretary's Commission on Achieving Necessary Skills, 1991).

The work that Albert Shanker, president of the American Federation of Teachers, reported in the *New York Times* (1988) summarizes it quite well. Shanker discussed research by Lauren Resnick of the University of Pittsburgh and Sue Berryman at Teachers College, Columbia. Resnick identified four ways that "out-of-context" school learning differs from the kind of learning that occurs and is required in the real world:

> First . . . students are expected to do things by themselves. But, in the real world, people usually work and solve problems as teams or by helping each other. Second, students are judged on how well they can do on their own—without notes, calculators and other aids. But doing well at work or in social situations depends on using mental and physical tools. Third, school learning is mostly about manipulating abstract symbols, but thinking or doing in the real world is mostly connected to concrete situations. Finally school learning is generalized, while outside learning is specific to a given context. (Shanker, 1988, p. E7)

The problem, according to Shanker, is that schools downplay the very skills that are most valuable on the work site. Shanker reports that Resnick concludes by citing mounting evidence which points to the possibility that very little can be transported directly from school to out-of-school use. Shanker (1988) further states that ". . . many youngsters don't see the point in playing the game of mastering material or skills that are so radically different from what people are doing in the outside world." Shanker continues by quoting Berryman, "[students may not be willing] to tolerate or make some sense out of a school-based experience . . . mainly because children see clearly that our schools offer a system of learning so completely at odds with the way people function in the outside world" (p. E7).

There is little question of the need to radically reform the total educational system in America. The question is whether or not we are willing to rethink the schooling process and reexamine the purpose of education.

Summary

The window of opportunity is now here for policy makers, educators, and society at large to critically examine whether the role of our educational system has drastically changed since the days of Plato's academe. Today everyone must be well prepared academically and technically and must be able to apply their knowledge and skills in the work force. The days of "check your brain at the gate" are past. As U.S. Secretary Reich and others have said many times, the days of unskilled high school graduates being able to obtain and maintain employment are gone. The antiquated, elitist, and "disconnected" educational system that might have been valid in ancient times is no longer appropriate.

So where do we go from here? As we try to reinvent an appropriate educational system, we need to keep in mind several basic facts:

- We have a 25% dropout rate in our secondary schools.
- At least half of the 50% of students who start college do not complete a four-year degree.
- Only 22% of the population complete a four-year degree.
- At least 50% of our youth are on educational pathways in which they fail, drop out, or are mismatched.
- Only 25% of the jobs by the year 2000 will require a bachelor's degree or above.
- Only 15% of the jobs by the year 2000 will be unskilled.
- Many of our youth do not see much relevancy in the schooling process and are bored and turned off by the whole process.
- At least 75% of young people have the ability to learn 75% of the jobs in society, if taught in an applied relevant manner.
- Cognitive scientists are saying people learn best through applied learning.

What else will it take to convince educators and society at large that radical reform of our educational system is imperative? As Clinchy says, "We need a vast, truly collaborative, root-and-branch effort to develop ways in which the education of *all* the students in our elementary and secondary schools and in our colleges and universities can be recontextualized. What our students learn—and the process by which they learn it—must be reconnected with and conducted largely out in that larger society" (Clinchy, 1994, p. 751). The philosophy that endorses one kind of education for a select group and a different kind for the rest is obsolete. To add work-based learning experiences to the preparation of those nonuniversity-bound students and do nothing to the college-bound curriculum will only continue to increase the dual system. College-bound students also need job skills and work-based learning. The number of university graduates not prepared for employment is increasing, and while we do not oppose liberal arts and the study of the classics for those who wish to do so, justification of the expense and sacrifice to the majority for the benefits of a minority is becoming increasingly suspect. The big leap is to change the thinking philosophically from the classical concepts of separation and creation of educated, learned minds for the few to an educational system that prepares everyone for the real world. To create an educated person who cannot get and hold a job probably has not helped the individual or society.

The single most important major paradigm shift is to realize there must be a connection between the schooling process and being able to make a living. It is now time to move away from the great sorting philosophy of Plato that we continue to perpetuate toward a success-oriented educational system for all. This means adopting the concepts of definition two of work-based learning (discussed in Chapter 2) and recognizing that we live in a work-oriented society. It is, therefore, logical that we muster all the forces we can to reinvent a new educational system for the twenty-first century.

 Now is the time to develop a system with a basic paradigm, philosophical foundation, and focus that people work in order to live and that there must be a positive "connectedness" between the schooling process and living productive lives for everyone.

References

American Council on Education. (1994, February 21–23). President Clinton's luncheon address at the annual meeting. Washington, DC.

Clinchy, E. (1994, June). "Higher Education: The Albatross Around the Neck of Our Public Schools." *Phi Delta Kappan*, 75(10), pp. 745–751.

Commission on the Skills of the American Workforce. (1990). *America's Choice: High Skills or Low Wages*. Rochester, NY: Author.

103rd Congress. (1994, May). School-to-Work Opportunities Act of 1994, sec. 2. H.R. 2884.

Council of Chief State School Officers. (1992). *Connecting School and Employment: Policy Statement 1991*. Washington, DC: Author.

Fiske, E. B. (1991). *Smart Schools, Smart Kids*. New York: Simon & Schuster.

Hoerner, J. L. (1994, February-March). "Work-Based Learning: The Key to School-to-Work Transition." *ATEA Journal, 21*(3), pp. 6–10.

Lester, J. (1994, January). "U.S. Adults Say High Schools Are Not Doing Enough to Help Students Develop Job Skills, Find Jobs and Plan Careers, Says New Gallup Survey." A paper and presentation given at the National Press Club, Washington, DC.

McLaughlin, A., Bennett, W. B., & Verity, C. W. (1988, July). *Building a Quality Workforce*. Washington, DC: U.S. Department of Labor.

Muffo, J. (1994, May). "Jobs, Jobs, Jobs, Quality Improvement in Action." *Academic Assessment Program*, Virginia Polytechnic Institute and State University, p. 1.

National Commission on Excellence in Education. (1983). *A Nation at Risk: The Imperative for Educational Reform*. Washington, DC: Author.

Pennington, H. (1992, October). "Youth Apprenticeship Program." A presentation at the National Tech Prep Conference. Chicago, IL.

Secretary's Commission on Achieving Necessary Skills. (1991, June). *What Work Requires of Schools: A SCANS Report for America 2000*. Washington, DC: U.S. Department of Labor.

Shanker, A. (1988, June 26). ". . . and the School-Student Connection." *New York Times*, p. E7.

Simon, R. I., Dippo, D., & Schenko, A. (1991). *Learning Work: A Critical Pedagogy of Work Education*. New York: Bergin & Garvey.

Thurow, L. C. (1993). *Head to Head*. New York: Warner.

William T. Grant Foundation Commission on Work, Family and Citizenship. (1988). *The Forgotten Half: Pathways to Success for America's Youth and Young Families*. Washington, DC: Author.

Wirth, A. G. (1992). *Education and Work for the Year 2000: Choices We Face*. San Francisco: Jossey-Bass.

Chapter **4**

Strategies for
Work-Based Learning

"The American philosopher, John Dewey, brought this idea [productive education] into the twentieth century consistently arguing that students learn best when productive experience is an integral part of education."
(Stern et al., 1994)

This chapter reviews a number of work-based learning strategies alluded to in Chapter 2. The discussion of each strategy is rather brief. Refer to the sources listed at the end of the chapter if you are interested in more details on a particular strategy. We are not recommending or supporting any one strategy over another, but rather providing this information as a foundation for further study. All of the strategies have their strengths and weaknesses. Future experimentation in education will narrow these options to the best ones. Our emphasis and support is based on making all education more relevant to life.

As a reminder, these strategies are only a part of work-based learning. Although very important, they are only a portion of the whole change that is needed in our educational system. The strategies described in this chapter emphasize definition one of work-based learning as discussed in Chapter 2. If these strategies were implemented into our educational system without any other changes, we would feel that great progress had been made. But the process of change would not be complete because these strategies do not completely encompass definition two of work-based learning as discussed in Chapter 2. Our view of the new educational system is more than reinventing or repackaging vocational education. Our view is much broader; it is based on systematically reforming the whole curriculum and education system.

Work-based learning strategies fall into two main categories: *job based* and *school based.* Although it is true that many job-based strategies also have school-based components, they are classified as job based because they are experienced predominantly in real job settings.

Because we believe work-based learning experiences need to integrate high-level academic and occupational instruction, it is not feasible for most employers to provide students with these work experiences. U.S. employers have a reputa-

28

tion for spending little on the training of their own employees. Most training dollars are spent on white-collar highly educated personnel. Therefore, if work-based learning is going to succeed broadly, school-based work experiences will have to be the predominant method of providing students with work experiences, at least until there is a major shift in attitude among business/industry leaders. The following is a list of the work experiences discussed in this chapter:

School-Based Work Experiences

1) school-based enterprises (SBEs)
2) career academies
3) customer service labs
4) job-shop labs
5) job-simulation labs
6) vocational/occupational labs
7) mock business/industry projects
8) senior and class projects

Job-Based Work Experiences

1) youth apprenticeship
2) cooperative education
3) clinical experiences
4) on-the-job training (OJT)
5) mentorship
6) internship
7) aligned work-study programs
8) school-linked summer employment
9) community service learning
10) business/education compacts

In addition, while not necessarily a strategy, there is a section on Tech Prep, a concept that uses many school-based and job-based work experiences. Tech Prep and other initiatives mesh many of these strategies. The 18 strategies discussed are not meant to be mutually exclusive. We fully expect that as these strategies evolve, there will be a meshing of the positive characteristics.

School-Based Work Experience
School-Based Enterprises (SBEs)

School-based enterprises are defined as "any activity through which students produce goods or services for sale to or use by people other than themselves" (Stern et al., 1994, p. 3). Although SBEs can be part of college preparation, they are typically part of a work-based curriculum. Several examples are child-care centers, restaurants, used car dealerships, supermarkets, hardware stores, and radio stations. As you can see from this brief list, the possibilities are endless. Any business outside of a school could possibly be a school-based enterprise. In rural areas, school-based enterprises can fill the gap in areas where employment is scarce.

While the activities the students perform in an enterprise may not exactly match what they will be doing upon graduation, the school-based enterprise brings a sense of reality to schools. Students view their academic education as more relevant to the SBE jobs than nonschool jobs (Stern et al., 1994).

School-based enterprises can generate revenue to support schools. The most obvious support is generating revenues to be used for purchasing equipment and other resources. However, there is a second and more subtle benefit. Enterprises can be used as incubators or start-up operations. These SBEs can be either turned over to local businesses or continued by students after graduation, resulting in economic development for the community. The addition of businesses increases tax revenues and benefits the school and the whole community.

Another of the subtle benefits of SBEs is the resulting positive school image. So often in our society a school is viewed as a building on so many acres where learning occurs. The SBE refocuses this viewpoint by mixing the community and school. The school is no longer restricted. The students pursue customers outside the school, contact suppliers, and even measure the competition. Competition is a sensitive area for local businesses. School-based enterprises need to assure their support by local businesses.

Career Academies

Career academies are simply schools within schools. Although few in number (less than 200), they have real promise when it comes to motivating the apathetic student. Career academies as an educational strategy have been around for centuries, but the majority of active models have been implemented in just the last decade.

Although career academies vary from location to location, the book *Career Academies* by David Stern, Marilyn Raby, and Charles Dayton (1992) lists several defining characteristics:

- It is a school within a school for grades 11 through 12, 10 through 12, or 9 through 12, run by a small team of teachers from various disciplines.

- It recruits students who volunteer for the program and demonstrate their commitment through an application process.

- It focuses on a career theme in a field in which demand is growing and good employment opportunities exist in the local labor market. The curriculum combines technical and academic content, usually through one technical and three academic classes each semester. Generic employability skills are also included. An academy keeps open students' options to attend college.

- Students are employed during the summer and (in some academies) part time during the school year in jobs related to their field of study.

- Employer representatives from the academy career field help plan and guide the program and are involved as speakers, field trip hosts, job supervisors, and sometimes mentors for individual students.

- Classes that are smaller than is typical in the high school, a system of motivational activities and rewards, and regular contacts with parents contribute to students' sense of membership in a caring community.

- A mixture of outside funding (in California through state grants), district backing, and employer contributions supports the program. Academies usually increase the cost of educating students somewhat, primarily through increased teacher costs and private sector involvement (pp. 14–15).

In career academies, academic and technical content are integrated and students learn by doing. The academic and technical or vocational teachers work together in planning programs. Teachers have more autonomy in developing, organizing, and coordinating the program as opposed to the role of the traditional teacher. To make the academy work, the teachers need common planning periods. The core staff typically consists of one technical and three academic teachers where one teacher assumes the lead or becomes the champion teacher. One of the teachers will often correspond with the parents keeping them aware of various activities. Students are motivated because they choose to join the academy. The familylike atmosphere, with students staying together in most of the same classes, also adds to the camaraderie; teachers get to know the students well over the period of the academy. These characteristics make the career academy appear ideal—parental and industry involvement combined with technical and academic content in a growing field, small classes in school, and outside employment experience while preserving the college option.

Customer Service Labs

The concept of customer service labs can be an excellent work-based learning strategy through which students can gain experience within the school-based setting. Customer service labs, although a type of school-based enterprise, have a broad range of possible applications. They are structured to provide a service to the outside public from the school lab. A common school-based service program is cosmetology/hair styling. Another example we found in one school was a small-engine repair service that was provided as part of a technology education program.

School-based customer service labs can provide excellent hands-on experience for students and be very realistically linked to the jobs in the career area found in the work environment of the community. It is important that customer service labs be operated like a real business so the students experience the breadth of activity appropriate for the occupation. They should experience the office side of the business and customer relations as well as the hands-on skill performance within the career. Just as any other school-based enterprise, customer service labs can be an excellent school-based strategy for work-based learning when such experiences are not readily available through job-based experiences.

Job-Shop Labs

Job-shop labs are vocational or occupational labs that take in outside work. Examples of this type of school-based work experience are auto mechanics labs and auto body labs that overhaul or do body work for automotive customers. Other examples are carpentry labs that build small utility buildings as well as houses on the school site or customer's lot and the welding labs that take in welding jobs. This kind of work-based learning experience is a form of school-based enterprise and incorporates the concepts of "learning by productivity." The concept of a job-shop lends itself to any school shop in high schools and community or technical colleges that have the capability to produce products or services that could be marketed. The job-shop strategy lends itself to a great variety of products and services and provides true hands-on work experience on the school campus. Like the customer service lab, it is important that such labs be operated as a business enterprise in order for students to have a real work experience comparable to that in a typical job setting.

Job-Simulation Labs

As in other school-based work experiences, the concept of job-simulation labs is to provide the hands-on experiences that simulate real job experiences as accurately as possible. The job-simulation lab experience includes organizing experiences and activities that duplicate or simulate the real thing. This strategy can be used in any career preparation pathway of study. One rather common use of this strategy is in office careers and business fields where office business is simulated.

In construction and building trade programs, job-simulation experiences could be constructing sections or components of buildings. In carpentry, for example, students can build a portion of a wall that contains a window and a door. In an electricity lab, students can run wire and hook up switches and fixtures on a simulated wall of a residential or commercial job. In machining, students might practice manufacturing parts similar to those of job-based machinists. In masonry and bricklaying, students can build walls, fireplaces, and so on. In the job-simulation strategy, the items constructed and practiced on are usually disassembled and the materials used again for future simulations.

The job-simulation strategy is an old work-based hands-on experience strategy used for years in many vocational education programs and has several advantages. The simulation experiences can be scheduled when they best fit in the program of study and are not dependent on all of the variables that exist in job settings. The experiences can be repeated as necessary. Because such experiences are usually conducted in a school lab, it is easy to relate the academic study to the hands-on experience. Math, science, and other academic classes can participate in such labs to support further integration between academic and occupational studies.

The job-simulation strategy has a wide application throughout many career fields of study. As education moves to providing more applied learning experiences, job simulation can be an excellent school-based strategy for hands-on experience.

Vocational/Occupational Labs

Vocational/occupational labs are simply traditional vocational education programs where occupational skills are taught. These labs, while still teaching occupational skills, are likely to move toward teaching broader skills such as critical thinking and communications. Also, the movement to integrate academics, especially math and science, into the vocational curriculum will result in the use of vocational labs as pedagogical tools. That is, the vocational labs will be used to show students the relevance of their academic courses.

Many have agreed that traditional vocational programs need reforming as much as the rest of education. However, traditional vocational programs have served as a good means for hands-on work-based experiences. The present vocational curricula needs to be updated to align with modern business/industry with emphasis on the skills needed in the various careers projected for the twenty-first century. Too frequently, traditional vocational programs have had students learning skills that are outdated. Also, coupled with the modern vocational/occupational labs of the future will be work-based experiences in job settings that parallel what the students are experiencing in the vocational labs. This could take place through co-op or summer internship experiences that further enhance the program. The modern vocational programs must also encorporate and integrate high-tech mathematics and science concepts that align with such future occupations. The United States must build on existing vocational programs to strengthen the schooling process. Well-developed modern vocational/occupational labs can play a major role in providing work-based learning experiences for an increasing number of our young people as we develop a viable school-to-work program for all of our youth.

Mock Business/Industry Projects

Mock business/industry projects are a form of simulated or contrived work-based experiences based on what actually goes on in the real job world. This strategy, like job-simulation labs, can be used for a wide variety of career areas. The mock business/industry project concept, however, works around projects more than lab-type activities.

The mock business/industry project strategy can be used in academic classrooms as well as occupational labs. A social studies class might develop a mock debate similar to some legal historical debate. Students, through role playing, can experience any number of business/industry negotiation activities. A technology education class might develop a mass-production project that allows students to experience the extensive complexities of a manufacturing business. In some mock business/industry projects products are actually produced. The concept again is to give the students a chance, through a project activity, to have as many real work experiences as can be incorporated into a project.

Senior and Class Projects

The strategy of senior and class projects is an excellent method for providing hands-on and relevant experiences that integrate academic learning with real experiences. The applications vary from individual projects entered into as seniors, for which purpose courses are integrated, to a project that the entire class takes on as a team.

For example, an individual could develop an entrepreneurial project that studies and incorporates all aspects (marketing, managing, financing, and manufacturing) of starting and operating a jewelry making business. In this case, the individual integrates classes in math, science, social studies, art, and language arts to develop the small business. This scenario would work for a marketing, business, arts, or metal working student. Another student might be in cabinet or furniture making or any number of career areas that lend themselves to this development format. The key is that the individual integrates his or her total educational experience into a related project.

The senior class project integrates several courses. For example, the class could develop a public relations and advertising campaign for the school consisting of brochures, videos, and other promotional materials. The various classes such as communications, printing, art, math, and science all work toward the schoolwide project. The advantages of class projects include learning to work as a team, integration across disciplines, hands-on experiences that align with a number of real jobs, and relevance for students' schooling experiences. Other benefits include employability attributes such as assuming responsibility, self-supervision, interpersonal skills development, communication skills, customer service experience, and broad curriculum application.

Senior and class projects can be an excellent strategy for providing a number of experiences beneficial to the future worker.

Job-Based Work Experiences

Youth Apprenticeship

In 1989 there were approximately 300,000 apprentices in the United States. The average age of these apprentices was 29 (Bailey, 1993). Less than 2% of the high school graduates in the United States enter apprenticeships (McKenna, 1992). Our current apprenticeship system is not structured for educating our youth. However, political support appears to be strong for the apprenticeship model. Apprenticeship legislation has been introduced in Congress in recent years with President Clinton and his administration strongly supporting the apprenticeship-type system.

The General Accounting Office, after studying the educational system in Germany, recommended expansion of apprenticeship-type programs to promote school-to-work transition. Youth apprenticeship, as we know it in the United

States, is not quite the same as an apprenticeship that is registered by a government. Youth apprenticeship is a term applied to a variety of school-to-work
programs that share only some of the characteristics of registered apprenticeship
programs. Youth apprenticeship can be defined as a program for students 16 or
older that integrates school instruction with on-the-job training and results in
both academic credentials and certification of mastery of work skills (Imel, 1993).

Our system of youth apprenticeship has many of the underpinnings of several
European educational systems: (1) coordination among employers, schools, labor,
and government; (2) integration of school and work-based learning; (3) certification of academic and occupational skill mastery; and (4) high skill and high
wage career routes that do not require a bachelor's degree (Imel, 1993). In
addition, a youth apprenticeship program should be structured to allow the
student to pursue postsecondary education.

In the document *Why America Should Develop a Youth Apprenticeship System,*
a five-step process was envisioned for the youth apprenticeship system in the
United States: (1) the curricula would expose those in the eighth through tenth
grades to various occupations; (2) tenth grade students would have a choice
between pursuing an apprenticeship or remaining on an academic track; (3) a
three-year apprenticeship would be developed starting in the eleventh grade;
(4) apprentices would be given a comprehensive test at the twelfth grade to
ensure competencies; and (5) at least 75% of the third year of apprenticeship
would be spent on the job. These suggestions, if implemented, would move the
United States toward a regulated governmental apprenticeship system. This
system, which is much like some European systems, would face tough questions
about tracking issues.

Youth apprenticeship can be defended as a worthwhile educational method
based on two primary arguments: (1) it is a system for moving non-college-
bound students into career employment; and (2) support of research in pedagogy
and learning theory (Bailey, 1993).

The movement of the schooling process into high-quality training gives the
student great potential for seeking a high-quality job. In apprenticeships, these
work experiences are more than menial job tasks. In the ideal model, the experiences add great value to the student's employability. Furthermore, increased
communication is developed between schools and industry.

The current organization of schools is seen as artificial by failing to teach
students many of the skills they will need in their jobs and lives (Bailey, 1993).
Some of the recent research suggests that traditional academic and vocational
schooling limits the full development of students' cognitive abilities (Bailey,
1993). The apprenticeship approach, however, is good both for teaching job-
related skills and developing cognitive abilities.

One of the big hurdles for youth apprenticeship is obtaining employer
involvement. In the past employers have not been enthusiastic about taking on
students even when subsidies have been offered. American employers prefer
employees with highly developed work habits. This attitude implies a track
record, which implies an older worker. The rejection by business and industry
of our youth implies that major incentives need to be offered to participating

businesses. A small inducement is not enough. Typically, business people do not believe their role is to educate high school youth. Because business people emphasize the bottom line, the incentive must be sizable; a good example is a tax incentive. This is not to say businesses are not charitable; however, if we want a major change in our educational system that would encompass greater involvement of business leaders, educational programs must be packaged to appeal to business and industry. We fear that the major paradigm shift resulting in more active business involvement in education is still a distant reality.

Can this strategy be implemented on a grand scale? Like many of the school-to-work methods discussed in this section, major philosophical changes in the way people view our educational system will have to occur.

Cooperative Education

Cooperative (co-op) education is a work-based learning technique that has great promise, but often falls short in practice especially at the secondary level. Ideally, co-op education entails a well-structured plan that integrates classroom knowledge with productive work experiences in a business/industry work setting. To help make the experience productive, communication between the teacher and the participating employer is crucial. A strong co-op experience will result in the student learning how the business world operates. At the high school level, students usually attend classes for half the day and work half the day. At the college or university level, the student often takes a break from school for a full semester to gain experience working in business or industry.

This general structure is very appealing; however, implementation often falls short of the ideal. Employers must be committed to adding value to the student rather than using the student solely for their own benefit. Many of the work experiences are simply jobs that students would have after school even if they were not in a co-op. In these instances, the cooperative experience merely reduces the amount of classroom learning and allows more time to work. Oftentimes the jobs are simply menial tasks where the student's learning is limited. To ensure the success of a co-op program, teachers must be active in facilitating the placement of students, which implies that teachers must develop relationships with businesspeople. The current lack of school-business relationships is a problem that must be overcome if co-ops are to be successful. The coordinating teacher is the vital link. Because these strong relationships are often lacking, students are left on their own to find their own co-op place of employment, which often leads to unsatisfactory experiences.

In spite of some of these criticisms, co-op education does often clarify career goals and result in greater self-confidence and increased motivation. There is still some question as to whether co-op students learn more, become more competitive, or find better jobs.

Properly implemented, cooperative education provides greater meaning to students' classroom learning, which, in turn, leads to a more motivated student.

These work-based experiences help the student understand work and what to expect in the world of work when they graduate.

With the movement toward a higher level of academic skills, the argument can be made that co-ops take time away from the classroom and the attainment of academic knowledge. This is the exact reason that the work-based experiences need to be highly productive and challenging. A strong program will develop the student's critical thinking skills and enhance rather than detract from a student's learning.

So, the question remains, are co-ops a viable work-based strategy? We think they can be, with proper support and commitment. Weak placement procedures will result in an artificial work-based experience. The key is placement. A strong placement depends on both the teacher and the industry participant. Like most programs, a co-op system is only as strong as its weakest link.

Clinical Experiences

The clinical work-based learning strategy is a common method that has been used in the health fields for years to provide work experiences. Most health occupations programs include clinical experiences at various stages of study whether in high school or postsecondary levels. The object of clinical experiences is to provide the student with hands-on work experiences in real job settings. They usually take place in hospitals and medical treatment facilities that provide actual experiences with real clients and patients. Clinical experiences are always conducted under very close supervision and linked closely with related classroom study. The clinical strategy works very well in most health-related occupations and has been used extensively in preparing most health professionals, for example, dental assistants and hygienists, nurse practitioners, and medical technicians.

On-the-Job Training (OJT)

On-the-job training (OJT) is often viewed as being unstructured and character-ized as "learn by doing" or "just pick it up" from an experienced employee (Jacobs, 1990). This unstructured method has received much criticism. Structured OJT, however, is the "one-on-one process of providing the knowledge and skills to perform a specific task within a job and consists of the following five features: (1) occurs in the actual workplace; (2) makes use of training objectives and plans; (3) requires the active involvement of a trainer; (4) uses printed materials and job guides; and (5) employs a systems approach" (Jacobs, 1990, p. 4).

OJT does not involve interaction between schools and work. However, the schools play a major role by ensuring recent graduates have the foundation to be attractive to employers for OJT.

The sole use of OJT for school-to-work transition implies that schools should primarily develop the academic skills of students and let industry develop the direct work-based skills. It is important to remember, however, that medium and small businesses are a large part of the economy and do not usually have the resources for extensive OJT.

OJT training does have the benefit of being directly relevant to the trainee. It is an active way of learning; theory is applied making the learning experience more motivational. OJT can be especially useful for students who struggle with bookish classroom teaching.

Apprenticeships and mentoring programs occur on the job but vary from OJT. Apprenticeships develop the skills of an individual in one skilled trade area whereas OJT emphasizes specific tasks within a job. Mentoring programs have a broader career orientation that emphasizes non-job-specific ideas such as the culture and the unwritten rules of the organization. OJT is not designed to expose new employees to organizational politics and climbing the corporate ladder.

OJT is more likely to fill a niche especially where training outcomes are similar with the expected outcomes of workers on that job. OJT training seems best for "skill" outcomes; off-site training is better for attaining "knowledge" (Jacobs, 1990). With the job market changing rapidly, knowledge and critical thinking skills are extremely important. OJT can be only a portion of the solution—one of the end points of school-to-work programs. However, before OJT takes place, there is much school-based educating and training that must be accomplished. New trainees must have the prerequisite knowledge and skills.

Mentorship

Mentoring can take many forms and varies widely in the degree of interaction between mentor and protégé. Some mentoring programs that occur as early as middle school act as a replacement for parents. In relation to work-based learning, the William T. Grant Foundation (1988) defines mentoring as ". . . an older more experienced person helping a younger one in a one-to-one relationship that goes beyond the formal obligations of a teaching or supervisory role" (p. 169).

The benefits of mentoring can be summarized as follows:

- Mentorship offers career exploration opportunities to experiment and learn firsthand from professionals about their chosen occupation;
- Mentorship programs are inexpensive (all mentors are volunteers);
- Mentorship immerses the student in the higher-order thought processes of the professional. In addition, students develop more motivation and find more meaning in their learning than students engaged in isolated fact-recall in classroom settings; and,
- It is in the relationship between content and context that a mentor can make the greatest contribution to student learning. (Smith & Rojewski, 1992, quoted from Backes, 1992).

Clearly, the mentoring process has great appeal and can be implemented with any school-to-work structure. However, obtaining enough qualified mentors can be a difficult task. Being a mentor takes a great commitment. For mentoring to be successful, the relationship between mentor and protégé typically needs to extend through at least a year. Furthermore, rapport and shared interests between the two participants is crucial (William T. Grant Foundation, 1988).

Internship

Internship is another strategy that is used to provide actual work experience as part of a career preparation program. While the term is common in the preparation of medical doctors, the same concept lends itself to other careers. The theory of an internship is to spend time obtaining field experience, usually near the end of the formal education or training program. Administration and supervision training programs, such as the AIT (Administrator-in-Training), often have an internship built into the training that is commonly used to prepare for a number of administrative positions. Universities often have internships as part of preparation in a number of professional areas.

Internships require jointly arranged field-based training between the business/industry career agency and the sponsoring educational agency. Such field-based internships provide actual hands-on experiences in the career setting under the supervision of a competent job supervisor. As the school-to-work transition process becomes of greater interest, the application of internship experiences will likely be more prominent.

Aligned Work-Study Programs

Traditionally work-study programs have been used as a means of financial aid to support students at both secondary and postsecondary levels. Generally, little, if any, relationship is formed between the work assignment and the area of study.

We are suggesting that work assignments could be developed with greater alignment and relationship to study programs as we move to making work-based learning more prominent in the school-to-work transition process. Most educational agencies have a great variety of work assignments that could be performed by students in various career pursuits. For example, students who are studying various office career fields could also perform office activities in the school offices as work-study students. Students who are studying restaurant and food preparation careers could work in the school kitchen as work-study students. The landscape horticulture students can work on school grounds maintenance and the construction trade career students can work in school building maintenance and physical plant jobs.

Work-study programs can also provide a wide variety of general employability skills that enhance all careers even if the specific tasks do not directly align with the area of career study. All young people need to learn general employability skills such as teamwork, punctuality, problem solving, communications skills, safety, interpersonal relationships, appropriate attitudes, and work ethics. Work-study programs could align and provide meaningful relationships between work assignments and career studies. We encourage educators to build such alignments where appropriate as work-based learning is expanded for all students.

School-Linked Summer Employment

With the expanded emphasis on work-based learning, school-linked summer employment is an ideal strategy to provide hands-on experiences for a large number of students. There is a wide variety of opportunity through which this strategy could be employed. As more industries recognize their role in forming partnerships with secondary and postsecondary educational agencies, they will be more willing to develop summer employment programs.

School-linked summer employment programs have several advantages as a work-based learning strategy. First, full-time work during the summer provides the student with an opportunity to experience full-time work. Second, the work setting provides meaningful work experiences. Third, when linked with the career area of study, the experience adds relevance to what is being studied in the school-based portion of the program. Fourth, most summer programs provide pay so a money incentive is built into the program as a motivation. Fifth, in many instances, companies such as Boeing, and Pratt and Whitney provide in-plant training internship experiences with their summer employment programs.

Community Service Learning

Community service learning links students with community service activities. Community service learning can be a win-win experience for students and the community. The community is not only immediately improved, but benefits from the development of a more socially conscious population. Students learn and practice broad work skills such as communications while possibly making contacts for future employment opportunities. Students are also exposed first hand to the issues and problems society faces. Helping others also can increase students' self-esteem.

Ideally, lessons from community service can be integrated into the classroom. For example, a class that cleans up a lake or recreational area may do an experiment on measuring pollution or study recycling in a science class and study the politics of environmental regulation in a social studies or government class.

Business/Education Compacts

Compacts between schools and the business community are rather complex, but the core of most compacts is structured to encourage student performance and school attendance. The benefit for the student is the promise of employment and financial support for pursuing postsecondary education. The idea is to develop a win-win situation for students and the business community. In essence, the implicit heart of the agreement from the business community viewpoint is simple: If you provide good students that are reliable, we will provide them with employment and support.

Schools commit to educating more job-ready as well as college-ready students. The business community agrees to hire more job-ready graduates and increase the financial aid to college-ready graduates. The difficulty occurs when these commitments are defined more specifically. It is common for the business community to request higher standards that school systems cannot meet.

The ideal development of compacts requires input from a cross section of the community. A compact's board should include students, parents, teachers, and government leaders at both the state and local levels. Detroit is one of the larger communities that has implemented compacts. Detroit's business community, the city and state governments, and the postsecondary community have all supported the compact. Financial support to compact schools, scholarships, summer jobs and learning experiences, mentors, and jobs for compact student graduates are some of the ways the various organizations have supported the compact system (Orr, 1993).

In a large school system such as Detroit's, each school must sign an agreement. This agreement will often state the school will implement a plan that will result in a highly skilled, reliable student. The exact plan to accomplish this is flexible; however, schools selected to be a member of the compact face competition from other schools. Additionally, students and parents usually sign an agreement stating they will reach the standards set by the compact. This arrangement is the reason some may argue that this method results in an elitist selection process rather than an inclusive system. The exclusion of individuals implies that compacts alone will not be the sole answer for school-to-work transition in the near future. However, it is a viable alternative that needs exploration and experimentation. Like all programs, the challenge is proper implementation and involvement. The plan the schools use to get the necessary skills for the students is very essential and will vary from location to location. Even though plans are important, the success or failure of a compact depends on student motivation. The compact concept relies heavily on students becoming motivated by seeing a direct link between their performance in school and their career and future. As long as students who go through the compact become employable in good jobs and business leaders truly support recent graduates, the compact shows great promise. However, if words are not backed up by actions, the compact process is likely to fail. Recessions and hard times cannot be excuses for not placing these students in satisfactory jobs. Trust is a key issue that cannot be underestimated.

Tech Prep

Tech Prep means different things to different people. It is not necessarily a four-year program that must lead to an associate's degree. Tech Prep does not even have to involve a community college. The law calls for two years of postsecondary education, which could include either an associate degree, apprenticeship, or a university that offers a two-year postsecondary certificate. Tech Prep is not exclusively for high-tech occupations. The Carl D. Perkins Act in section 347(3) defines Tech Prep in the following way:

> [T]he term tech-prep education program means a combined secondary/postsecondary program . . . consist(s) of 2 [or 4 years as amended by STWOA, 1994] years of secondary . . . and 2 years of higher education, or an apprenticeship program of at least 2 years following secondary instruction with a common core of required profi-

ciency in mathematics, science, communications, and technologies designed to lead to an associate degree or certificate in a specific career field . . . and leads to ". . . effective employment placement or transfer of students to 4-year baccalaureate degree programs. . . ." (*Congressional Record*, 101st Congress, 2nd Session, September 25, 1990, pp. 790–791)

Tech Prep is "an articulated program of 2 years [or 4 years] high school and 2 years postsecondary preparation which includes a common core of math, science, communications, and technologies designed to lead to an associate degree or certificate in a specific area" (Hoerner, 1992–1993, p. 12). In practice, there is no consistent formula for all Tech Prep programs. Each site seems to have its own interpretation of the act. Implementation of Tech Prep at most locations is in its infancy so it is difficult to predict accurately how the programs will unfold.

Under Tech Prep, the core academic courses emphasize practical application of academic material and are often taught in a hands-on manner. Although there is some debate about its academic level, the material is intended to be as rigorous as regular academic courses. There are two main approaches to teaching these academic courses: (1) as stand-alone courses, and (2) as modules within the current academic courses. There are many commercially developed stand-alone applied academic courses. Applied Mathematics, Applied Biology/Chemistry, and Principles of Technology are just a few examples of curriculum that is available. These courses often serve as complete substitutes to the traditional academic course. The second method of weaving applied materials into current academic courses is also common. For example, a traditional English course may integrate real-world communications in writing or speaking assignments for the class. Because most of these teachers have a purely academic background, they are still struggling with obtaining applied knowledge and teaching methodology. In these instances, the commercially developed materials are extremely valuable. Some advanced Tech Prep programs integrate course content among or between courses. This, of course, requires significant leadership by administration and dedicated teamwork by both the academic and vocational teachers.

The technologies portion of Tech Prep consists of career clusters. For example, in Virginia there are five career clusters: (1) Agriculture, Environment, and Natural Resources; (2) Business and Marketing; (3) Health, Human, and Public Services; (4) Engineering and Industrial Technologies; and (5) Communications, Arts, and Media. These hands-on occupationally specific clusters integrate academic knowledge into applied courses.

It is true that Tech Prep is interpreted and implemented in different ways throughout the country. Although there are problems with this, there are also benefits. Tech Prep is designed to be flexible to meet the demands of the local market. In the Northwest, aerospace technology may be emphasized; agriculture may be stressed in the Midwest. This flexibility is what helps students develop the necessary skills to be employable in the local labor market. If implemented properly, students are obtaining strong academic yet broad educations to remain flexible in future career choices.

Tech Prep is not a panacea for all school-to-work transition, but it has many positive characteristics. As this initiative continues, more consensus about the components of Tech Prep programs should emerge. Regardless of the term used, many of the characteristics of Tech Prep are likely to continue in various forms.

Summary

Traditional vocational education is under attack as evidenced by the trend to eliminate many vocational education departments at universities. Many of the strategies outlined here are new methods for delivering traditional vocational education. It can be argued that the curriculum in secondary schools is moving to higher academic requirements. The concept of keeping vocational separate from academic is disappearing. It is important to emphasize that these strategies are expected to help develop students' academic skills. That is, these strategies are both work-based strategies and pedagogical strategies to help students understand the relationship of academic and vocational or occupational skills. The movement in vocational education is to have students obtain broader skills that are transferable in the changing world. Such skills as critical thinking and communications are important goals, as is lifelong learning. This implies that our educational system needs to teach students how to learn on their own.

Vocational education as we have known it in the past is not likely to continue in the future. We hope the lines of academic and vocational education will be blurred because it is important to avoid tracking. There will always be critics believing these strategies are simply forms of tracking students or designed for the low-achieving student. These strategies need to be formed to attract *all* students. It must be clear that all strategies should be flexible to allow students to obtain further education. This flexibility is an important component of the School-to-Work Opportunities Act of 1994. If students who plan to pursue a four-year degree do not participate, these strategies are likely to be considered the new dumping ground, merely the replacement of vocational education.

The strategies just discussed provide many exciting opportunities for educators. This is clearly a time of exploration for many of the educational systems throughout the country. Each strategy has its own unique barriers to becoming successful. The further away from traditional education and the higher the demand on industry, the greater the struggle may be to implement such strategies. Without the support of local administrators, these strategies have no chance of success. This is why the philosophical changes discussed in Chapter 3 are so important. Industry support and participation are critical for all work experiences and obviously mandatory for site-based work experiences. Presently, industry is not willing or able to participate to any great extent in site-based work experiences. This implies two main points. First, school-based work experience strategies will be the primary means of implementation of the School-to-Work Opportunities Act. Second, philosophical systemic changes are not only needed by educators, but also industry leaders if site-based work experiences are to become significant. As we discuss in Chapter 8, which focuses on the role of business, this philosophical change will come about only if there are incentives for industry to become involved in the educational process.

Work-based learning strategies, whether school based or job based, provide the schooling process with creative methods for delivering hands-on experience for all students; however, we must not forget the importance of systemically reforming the total curriculum and educational system in order to meet the challenges of the twenty-first century.

References

Bailey, T. (1993). "Can Youth Apprenticeship Thrive in the United States?" *Educational Researcher* (April), pp. 4–10.

Congressional Record, 101st Congress 2nd Session (1990, September 25). The Carl D. Perkins Vocational and Applied Technology Act Amendments of 1990.

Hoerner, J. L. (1992–1993). "Breaking the Mold: Tech Prep and the New Paradigm." *ATEA Journal 20*(2), pp. 11–15.

Imel, S. (1993). *Youth Apprenticeship: Trends and Issues Alerts* (ED 359 375). Washington DC: Office of Educational Research and Improvement.

Jacobs, R. L. (1990). *Structured On-the-Job Training.* Training and development research report (ED 326 641). Columbus: Ohio State University.

McKenna, J. (1992). "Apprenticeships: Something Old, Something New, Something Needed." *Industry Week* (Jan. 20), pp. 14–20.

Orr, M. (1993). "Urban Regimes and School Compacts: The Development of the Detroit Compact." *Urban Review 25*(2), pp. 105–120.

Smith, C. L., & Rojewski, J. W. (1992). *School-to-Work: Alternatives for Educational Reform* (ED 354 303). Athens University of Georgia.

Stern, D., Raby, M., & Dayton, C. (1992). *Career Academies: Partnerships for Reconstructing American High Schools.* San Francisco: Jossey-Bass.

Stern, D., Stone, J., III, Hopkins, D., McMillion, M., & Crain, R. (1994). *School-Based Enterprise: Productive Learning in American High Schools.* San Francisco: Jossey-Bass.

William T. Grant Foundation Commission on Work, Family and Citizenship. (1988). *The Forgotten Half: Pathways to Success for America's Youth and Young Families.* Washington, DC: Author.

Chapter 5

Career Counseling and the Individual Career Development Plan

"If there is a key to forging the connection between school and work it lies in providing career counseling throughout the school years."
(Billings, 1993)

A Consensus for Change in Career Counseling

If one were to identify one of the major weaknesses of the current educational system in the United States, it would be the absence of adequate career counseling. Practically every article, research study, book, and document addressing restructuring and reforming education emphasizes the need to expand and change the career counseling function. R.I. Lerman (1994) says, "[Y]oung people are poorly informed about occupations. School counselors have little time or capability to be effective with the non-college bound." And he further states that even the "U.S. Employment Service does little to encourage young people to learn about the tasks involved in various occupations and the skills required" (p. 21).

In his book *Opening Minds, Opening Doors* (1993), Dan Hull discusses that most young people move through high school and beyond with little clear idea about what they want to achieve in their careers. Many do not understand the basic concepts of a career. He says that schools do not systematically provide enough practical career information and guidance. "The elementary years are not too early to begin exposing children to different groups of careers or career areas, introducing the concept of the career ladder, and explaining the educational requirements for entry and advancement in a career. The middle and high school years should feature opportunities for career exploration and curricula that connect what is learned in the classroom to what is needed at work" (Hull, 1993, p. 11).

Numerous other studies have emphasized this great dearth of effective career counseling in the current schooling process. The 1993 study titled *Losing Generations* presented one of the most profound descriptions of current ineffective school career counseling, quoting from the RAND study by Haggstrom, Blaschke, and Shavelson (1991):

> [M]any if not most high school seniors have only vague notions as to where they are headed and how they will get there . . . lacking clear cut objectives and being subject to myriad factors that can deflect them from their pursuits, many will experience numerous diversions and setbacks before they find their niches in the adult world. (Commission on Behavior Social Sciences and Education of the National Research Council, 1993, p. 127)

The Council of Chief State School Officers (CCSSO) 1991 policy statement included, "We support changes in schools that promote a quality primary and secondary education with early orientation to work that enables all young people to pursue continued education and challenging employment" (CCSSO, 1992, p. 2).

A consensus is developing rapidly in the literature and among practitioners that the basic building blocks of an effective career preparation system must include increased career exposure and counseling (Kazis, 1993). We must place new emphasis on career education that should become part of the K–12 curriculum so our children have a rich understanding of the industries that drive our economy and the occupational opportunities within them. Guidance counseling in our schools should be about careers, not just college choices.

Former secretary of labor Ray Marshall and Marc Tucker in their book *Thinking for a Living* (1992) advocate career exposure for young people built into school curricula from the first year of grade school through at least the end of compulsory education. It is becoming increasingly obvious that such career counseling and development also needs to improve at the college and university level. The findings of the College Needs Assessment Survey reflect that 60% or more of undergraduates rate the need for learning about job opportunities in their career area of interest among the top four areas of educational and personal needs (Muffo, 1994). An article in the *Chronicle of Higher Education* (1994) by Ben Gose also reflected the expanded need for more career development in his comments about the need for liberal arts students to have internships and work experience.

The need for greater career counseling and development is summarized very well by the Gallup Survey that was reported at the National Press Club in Washington, D.C., January 11, 1994. The September-October 1993 survey was a sample of approximately 171.2 million adults 18 years of age and older. The following rather significant findings were reported at the Press Club by Juliette Lester (1994), executive director of the National Occupational Information Coordinating Committee regarding the need for better career counseling in our schooling process:

- 72% of the working adults in the United States say they wish they had been given more information about their career options.
- 64% of U.S. adults say that schools are not doing enough to help young people find jobs.

- 57% say schools are not doing enough to help students use occupational information.
- 60% of U.S. adults think public schools are not devoting enough attention to helping students who do not plan to attend college to develop the skills they need to find jobs.

The Gallup survey also revealed the extent to which various individuals sought advice about career options from school and college counselors:

- Only 5% of the non–high school graduates report they talked to a school counselor about career options.
- Only 15% of the high school graduates talked to counselors about careers.
- 52% of college graduates sought some counselor assistance.

These survey data further support the recognition and increasing awareness of the critical need to develop an extensive career counseling function in the schooling process. When approximately three fourths of adult society wish they had been given more information about career options, it is imperative that policy makers, educators, parents, and society at large recognize the importance of changing the system.

Much of the absence of career counseling has been a result of an ongoing philosophy that has not traditionally supported a relevant connection between the schooling process and the world of work. Administrators, teachers, and counselors still do not believe making connections is important. Unfortunately, the American educational system is still suffering from, as D. Parnell (1994) has discussed, the tendency of the American educational system to favor the concept of a "classical subject-matter education in the tradition of the Greek philosopher Plato over the more practical problem solving approach favored by Aristotle" (p. 37). Parnell further argues that a body of leaders in this country still holds that the term *education* refers only to the development of the intellectual proficiencies and the dissemination of knowledge. Whereas others hold to a broader definition that includes application of knowledge to real-life situations. This dichotomy in educational philosophy still remains a source of the continuing dilemma over the appropriate purposes of education. We believe the time is overdue to resolve this dilemma, which has contributed greatly to the absence of adequate career counseling. Without career information, counseling, and direction, students are encouraged (even expected) to choose content-oriented education with little direction, application, or relevancy to their future.

What Is Needed Now?

It is obvious that we need an extensive and comprehensive career counseling function throughout the schooling process. The School-to-Work Opportunities Act (STWOA) of 1994 defines career guidance and counseling as follows:

[T]he body of subject matter and related techniques and methods organized for the development in individuals of career awareness, career planning, career decision making, placement skills, and knowledge and understanding of local, state, and national occupational, educational, and labor market needs, trends, and opportunities . . . that assist individuals in making and implementing informed educational and occupational choices . . . and . . . that aid students to develop career options. . . . (103rd Congress, 1994, p. 8)

The act also includes as its twelfth purpose,

. . . to expose students to a broad array of career opportunities, and facilitate the selection of career majors, based on individual interests, goals, strengths, and abilities. . . . (103rd Congress, 1994, p. 7)

Clearly, the STWOA argues for the educational system to integrate career development into schools. In elementary school, students should be exposed to a variety of careers so they can begin thinking about their futures and obtaining an understanding of how knowledge is applied. As students move into high school, counselors need to take a more assertive role in helping students select a potential career. Emphasis should be placed on students' interests, goals, strengths, and abilities rather than focusing on college as the only route to success.

In her book *Tech Prep & Counseling: A Resource Guide*, Chew (1993) suggests that major attitude changes will have to occur so parents and educators recognize and accept that a four-year degree is not the only pathway toward career success. Counselors can play a major role in increasing the awareness level of students, parents, and the community. Chew (1993) provides the following suggestions for methods counselors can use to enhance "career awareness" (p. 148):

- Implement a developmental guidance model for K–12.
- Provide all students with interest and aptitude assessments.
- Provide schoolwide activities that promote the awareness of technical career opportunities.
- Provide students with information about community or technical colleges.
- Give attention to women, minorities, and students with special needs, and provide them with knowledge of opportunities.
- [Provide] . . . access to appropriate materials and resources that explain the options of Tech Prep and technical careers.
- Help students develop a portfolio that summarizes their educational and experiential credentials.
- Utilize career planners.

Career counseling is not, however, the exclusive function of counseling and guidance personnel. In keeping with the scope of career guidance and counseling as defined in STWOA, career counseling becomes a schoolwide function. Therefore, teachers and administrators, in addition to counselors, have a role to play. Career counseling must be within the central theme and focus of the schooling process. It must be firmly embedded in *the knowledge/learning imparted to every student from the beginning of schooling that maintains a theme or focus that people work to live and that there is a positive connectedness between the schooling process and living productive lives* (definition two; see Chapter 2). This would mean that every educator is helping the students see the connections and relationships between what is being learned and their career options and directions.

The career development process should follow and permeate the total educational system. This requires radical philosophical change in our schooling process and requires the basic paradigm of education to be built around the mission of preparing all students for *further learning* and *productive employment.* When this becomes the basic philosophical mission of education, the career guidance process should provide the information, experiences, and activities that assist individuals in making and implementing informed educational and occupational choices. Therefore, one of the major keys to the new connections lies within the career counseling and development process.

Career Development Plans

In a work-oriented society education ought to be goal oriented and lead to a practical outcome. All young people need to begin early to think how they are going to function as self-supporting, productive individuals and put food in their mouths, clothes on their backs, and a roof over their heads.

The schooling process now needs to include the concept of Career Development Plans (CDP) for each and every student including the college bound. After all, we have IEPs (Individual Education Plans) for special needs students. Increasingly, there are various career counseling systems being developed such as the Career Development Portfolio Project of the National Occupational Information Coordinating Committee (NOICC); the "Get a Life" portfolio system developed by NOICC and the American School Counselor Association; and the Career Quest project of the Dothan City Schools in Dothan, Alabama. The various systems tend to follow the portfolio format with the inclusion of a process which leads to awareness and exploration of the students' career interests as well as their aptitudes and abilities. The various processes lead ultimately to matching interests and abilities that provide focus for the career development and preparation process. That, in turn, leads to being prepared to be a productive, self-supporting, contributing member of society.

The Individual Career Development Plan (ICDP)

An ICDP, developed by Hoerner (1993), is a career development portfolio or plan that assists individuals throughout their career exploration and preparation and links their studies to their future goals. The ICDP should begin at about the third grade and continue through the completion of the schooling process. It would help keep all students, including the college bound, focused on their futures as they explore and become more aware of their career options. As the concept of career majors expands for all students, the ICDP will provide greater focus.

The ICDP is for all students—the future engineer, physician, lawyer, business leader, nurse, machinist, carpenter, and computer technician. We know many readers at this point are thinking that young people cannot be asked to make career decisions in the elementary grades. Marshall and Tucker (1992), as we previously stated, suggested career exposure be built into the curriculum starting with the first year of grade school. Many others allude to early career awareness also. There seems to be an American tendency to keep young people from career decisions. Hamilton (1994) stated, "In this country, there is a visceral fear of tracking that translates into a message that any road can take any kid any- where. . . . If you don't know where you are going, any road will take you there" (pp. 26–27). This sort of thinking, that too often permeates our schooling process from elementary school through at least high school, has devastating results for a significant number of our young people as well as their families. This lack of direction and focus makes education a process without purpose instead of a goal-oriented direction for achievement with meaning and rewards for hard work. Again, this is why career guidance and counseling is so critical. Nontracking, which parents and educators seem to favor so strongly, is a form of tracking. This lack of direction leads to the general education track, which has no direction, or to dropping out of high school. For others, it means continuing an educational process with little relevance, which results in the pursuit of a college degree by default in the absence of awareness of other viable options. Too often the university becomes a very expensive exploratory institution that produces graduates with bachelor's degrees who still do not know what they want to do.

An Individual Career Development Plan that starts in the third grade only serves as a beginning for a structure that ultimately hones and focuses on a direction that adds relevance to the schooling process. The ICDP also provides educators the opportunity to relate learning to their students' potential futures, which can greatly add motivation and reason for learning. The challenge, how- ever, in this concept is that teachers would need to get beyond content dissemina- tion and move to knowing actual real-world applications.

It has been argued that elementary youth do not know what they want to do. Of course this is true; however, this does not prevent elementary students from choosing several potential career areas of interest and learning how course content is applied to such careers. There is no question that the majority of students will change career interests many times. In the early stages, the ICDP is a great exploratory tool. The purpose of the ICDP is not to lock students into careers but rather to provide focus that people work to live and that there is a connection between the schooling process and their futures.

The ICDP format is a career portfolio or notebook that accompanies individ- ual students throughout their schooling, continually being revised and refined as career development takes place. Again, the key is that the ICDP serves as a tool around which students relate their program of study for their career major throughout their schooling including postsecondary preparation when appro- priate. Two very important points need to be stressed. First, the ICDP belongs to the student. The more connected they feel to their career development plan, the more the ICDP can contribute to their self-esteem and motivation. It does not belong to the counseling office or third grade teacher or anyone else. Second, the ICDP is not an assignment to be corrected or graded by an adult passing judgment.

The following 16 components and content categories are recommended for ICDPs. As the individual student matures, it is expected that the various sections would be modified and expanded. Following is a suggested format divided into sections for an ICDP (Hoerner, 1994):

1) *Essays on "What I Want to Be."*

2) *Description of process for becoming that worker.* The student will write a brief narrative about the process for preparing for the career(s) of their choice. As they mature, this section will be greatly expanded.

3) *Summary of career aptitudes and interest tests.* Include all career aptitude and interest assessments as the student progresses through the schooling process.

4) *Career Information.* Expand over time and include such elements as (1) job-specific information; (2) career/job description; (3) traits and competencies required in job/career, and so on.

5) *Education and training requirements for career/job.* Students need to consider the type of education and training required: (1) community college; (2) apprenticeship; (3) university; (4) business/industry training; (5) military training; or (6) other sources of preparation.

6) *Costs for education and training and sources of financing.* (1) scholarships, (2) industry, (3) armed services, and (4) other.

7) *Summaries of interviews with workers in career choices.* Students at all levels, even third and fourth graders, can talk to family and relatives about their careers. Talking to people who do the kind of work they are interested in pursuing is of utmost importance.

8) *Summaries of mentoring experiences.* Although third graders might not be involved in mentoring experiences, older students should have several mentor experiences at various points throughout their career decision-making process.

9) *Part-time work experiences.* Briefly describe various kinds of part-time work.

10) *Co-op experiences.* Briefly describe any co-op experiences.

11) *Other contacts and experiences with career interests.* Other experiences not included in sections 7, 8, 9, or 10, for example, apprenticeship experiences.

12) *Career projections.* (1) salaries, (2) promotional opportunities, (3) future projections.

13) *Locations for career employment.* This section is for geographical awareness. Is the career of interest only located in Alaska or Australia?

14) *Career opportunity listings and notices.* Collect clippings from newspaper ads, journals, and magazines relating to various careers of interest.

15) *Other career characteristics.* Discussions and materials that relate to (1) seasonal work; (2) individual or teamwork; (3) self-employment opportunities; (4) hazards; (5) effects of economy, and so on.

16) *Visual descriptions of career/jobs.* Elementary students may collect pictures and illustrations of workers in the careers being considered. Again, this section will expand and change as the student matures and the plan materializes.

These 16 sections are suggested as a guide. We recommend that they be adapted to the individual student's needs. We want to emphasize the ICDP is the student's career portfolio and represents their road map to their futures. The more they "own" their ICDP, the more responsibility they will take in planning their own lives. They should be encouraged to take their ICDP notebooks to their various classes, and teachers should ask about the Individual Career Development Plan and relate lessons to students' future plans. For example, math teachers can relate various lessons to individual students' career directions and ICDPs.

Summary

As we stated earlier, one of the most important keys to successful school-to-work transition is comprehensive career counseling and development for *all* students. The literature is replete with consensus on the importance of our schooling from kindergarten through university providing comprehensive career guidance and development for all of our young people.

However, to provide the much needed career counseling and guidance we must first get all educators to recognize the need for positive connections between the schooling process and students' futures. We believe career counseling is one of the most important links in our schools to encourage, support, and facilitate this connection between school and work.

Figure 5.1 contains the seven roles we believe should be carried out as part of the counseling function for the school-to-work initiative.

Figure 5.1
The Counselor's Role

1) Foster a climate conducive to everyone preparing to be productive, independent, and contributing members of society.

2) Be the catalyst for the school-to-work transition initiative.

3) Stop the dual track system mentality of college bound versus career bound.

4) Launch Individual Career Development Plan (ICDP) for all students.

5) Establish comprehensive career information systems.

6) Provide leadership for in-service activities to shift the emphasis toward career-oriented education.

7) Build extensive linkages between business/industry and education.

Comprehensive career counseling including a well-structured ICDP for all students will provide one of the major links for connecting the schooling process to each student's future as he or she works toward becoming an independent, productive, self-supporting, and contributing member of society.

References

Billings, J. A. (1993). "Steps for School-to-Work System." A public relations pamphlet from the Washington State Superintendent of Public Instruction Office.

Chew, C. (1993). *Tech Prep & Counseling: A Resource Guide*. Madison: Center on Education and Work, University of Wisconsin.

Commission on Behavioral and Social Sciences and Education of the National Research Council. (1993). *Losing Generations: Adolescents in High-Risk Settings*. Washington, DC: National Academy Press.

103rd Congress. (1994, May). School-to-Work Opportunities Act of 1994. H.R. 2884.

Council of Chief State School Officers. (1992). *Connecting School and Employment: Policy Statement 1994*. Washington, DC: Author.

Gose, B. (1994, May 18). "More Jobs: Liberal Arts Graduates Still Find Dim Prospects." *Chronicle of Higher Education XL*(37), pp. A28, A30.

Hamilton, S. (1994). "Democratization, Technological Change and Global Competition." In *Building a System to Connect School and Employment*. Washington, DC: Council of Chief State School Officers and American Youth Policy Forum.

Hoerner, J. (1993). "An Individual Career Development Plan for All Students." A concept paper. Virginia Polytechnic Institute and State University, Blacksburg, VA.

Hoerner, J. (1994). "Urge Kids to Get an Early Start on Careers." *Vocational Education Journal*, 69(3), p. 54.

Hull, D. (1993). *Opening Minds, Opening Doors: The Rebirth of American Education*. Waco, TX: CORD Communications.

Kazis, R. (1993). "Improving the Transition from School-to-Work in the United States." Washington, DC: American Youth Policy Forum, Competitiveness Policy Council, and Jobs of the Future.

Lerman, R. I. (1994, March). "Reinventing Education: Why We Need the School-to-Work Initiative." *Vocational Education Journal* 69(3), pp. 20, 21, 45.

Lester, J. N. (1994, January). "U.S. Adults Say Schools Are Not Doing Enough to Help Students Develop Job Skills, Find Jobs and Plan Careers, Says New Gallup Survey." A paper and presentation given at the National Press Club, Washington, DC.

Marshall, R., & Tucker, M. (1992). *Thinking for a Living: Education and the Wealth of Nations*. New York: Basic Books/HarperCollins.

Muffo, J. (1994, May). "Jobs, Jobs, Jobs, Quality Improvement in Action." *Academic Assessment Program*, p. 1.

Parnell, D. (1994). *LogoLearning: Searching for Meaning in Education*. Waco, TX: Center for Occupational Research and Development, Inc.

Chapter 6

Career Majors for All–
Are We Ready?

"One reason people are so dissatisfied with modern education is that we have failed to match in any systematic way the goals of education with the competencies required to function successfully in our modern society."
(Parnell, 1994)

The United States can no longer afford an educational system that continues to be disconnected from the real world. In many of today's classrooms, hands-on, contextual, applied learning is absent, and little effort is made to connect what students are learning to the world in which they will spend their adult lives.

To frame this chapter, three major premises set the direction that education needs to take:

1) The changing needs of the American work force are greatly impacting our educational system.

2) The purpose of education as we approach the twenty-first century must now change to meet those needs.

3) Career majors for all students will provide purpose and meaning for the schooling process in this work-oriented society.

Changing Needs of America's Work Force

This is not intended as a comprehensive review of the changing needs of the work force in this country. The specific details we leave to Marshall and Tucker (1992), *Thinking for a Living*; Thurow (1993), *Head to Head*; and Reich (1992), *The Work of Nations*; as well as others who have traced comprehensively the need for such changes. They discuss the shift in the U.S. economy, the rapidly changing technology, and the need for a highly skilled work force if the United States is going to stay globally competitive in the international marketplace. While some businesses may not currently be having a problem in recruiting qualified workers, there may indeed be an increasing shortage of skilled workers as technology evolves. Figure 6.1 graphically displays the changing needs of the work force as we approach the twenty-first century. In the last 50 years we have moved from approximately two thirds of the work force being unskilled to the present where projections for the near future indicate approximately two thirds of the work force will need to be skilled.

All one needed during the early twentieth century was a strong back and the willingness to work to make a living in America, where the work force was organized and managed primarily by applying the Frederick Winslow Taylor model. Taylor's model was conceived as an efficient way to organize mass production with a large population of low skilled, uneducated workers. The basic premise of the system was to break complex jobs down into a myriad of simple rote tasks, which the worker then repeated with machine-like efficiency. Taylor's ideas were designed on the assumption (in the early 1900s) that educated workers would be hard to find. The system was managed by educated supervisors and managers who established elaborate administrative organizations and structures to control a large number of workers (Commission on the Skills of the American Workforce, 1990).

Most employees under the Taylor model did not need to be educated. The only requisite was to be reliable, steady, and able to follow instructions. The bosses and managers did the thinking. The workers only needed to supply the grease for the wheel—and "leave their brain at the gate." As the book *America's*

Figure 6.1

The Changing Needs of the American Work Force

Reprinted from Brustein, M., & Mahler, M. (1994). *AVA Guide to the School-to-Work Opportunities Act.* Alexandria, VA: American Vocational Association. Reprinted by permission.

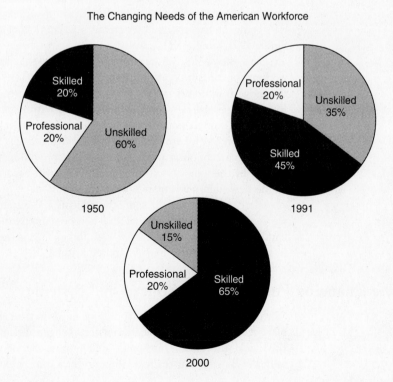

The Changing Needs of the American Workforce

Choice discusses, America prospered greatly during the 1950s and 1960s with the Taylor model. The United States embraced the Taylor system more firmly than any other country. This system helped make our country rich and the largest manufacturer with the biggest middle class of any country in the world. The Taylor system continues to define the job expectations of many workers.

As the new century approaches, the old work organization is becoming less appropriate for a high-wage nation. High-speed communication and transportation make it possible to produce durable goods and services anywhere in the world. Modern machinery and production methods can be combined with fewer low-wage workers to drive costs down.

Companies in the United States and other high-wage countries are beginning to adopt another style of work. The new work organization is reducing bureaucracy by downsizing and giving greater responsibility to lower level workers. Front-line workers are being asked to take over many of the tasks that lower and middle management used to perform. They are being asked to use judgment and make decisions rather than follow rote procedures. The modern worker is being asked to participate in quality control and production scheduling as well as enter into many other management decisions. Tasks formerly performed by dozens of unskilled individuals are now performed by fewer individuals organized around highly skilled teams. As a result, we are seeing new forms of work organizations that are demanding a highly skilled and well-educated worker who is now expected to think. As stated in *SCANS* (1991), "a well-developed mind, a passion to learn, and the ability to put knowledge to work are the new keys to the future of our young people, the success of our businesses, and the economic well-being of the nation" (Secretary's Commission on Achieving Necessary Skills, 1991, June, p. 1).

The new work organizations are driving the demand for highly skilled workers. There is no question that different companies are at different stages in the move to a highly skilled work force. But the critical point is not so much where we are now, but where we are headed. Without an educated, highly skilled work force, many companies have little choice except to settle into a low-wage organization. As we approach the twenty-first century, we still face the problem of having a schooling process that is not providing the education and skills needed by the majority of our students who will become the front-line workers in the new high-performance work organization.

Here then lies the dilemma the educational system is currently facing. Are we ready to develop a system that is about preparing people to be effective employees in the new American work force? This is the question that must now be addressed by policy makers and educators.

The Changing Purpose of the Educational System

With the dramatic change in work force needs in the last 50 years, the traditional management model for education will no longer suffice. As discussed throughout this book, the basic philosophy and purpose of our educational system must radically change. The reality is that America cannot expect to have a world class work force without an educational system that incorporates purpose, strategies, methodologies, and expectations which result in all students being well prepared for their futures.

Never has the nation's educational system been at such a critical crossroads as today. It has been asked by many: Do we want to continue to commit our resources to providing a good education for a few or do we want to provide a meaningful education for *all?* This is the critical question now being faced by policy makers, educational leaders, teachers, and society at large. Renate and Geoffrey Caine, in their book *Making Connections: Teaching and the Human Brain* (1991), said it well: "If students are to become genuinely more proficient, more capable of dealing with complexity and change, more highly motivated, and more capable of working both autonomously and with others, then we have no choice but to teach for meaningfulness" (p. 172).

One of the major challenges for educational leaders is to develop purposeful goals at all levels of education. Parnell (1994) discusses how few instructors and administrators in our educational institutions are currently focusing on the goals and purposes of their schools or colleges. During the last couple of years, when addressing many groups of educators at state and national conferences, we have asked this: "How many teachers have, in the last six months, participated in a professional meeting to discuss the purpose of education?" We found that most teachers responded negatively. Although this has been a very informal survey of approximately 2000 educators in approximately 20 states, it does appear that very few of them are devoting much time to discussing the purpose of the schooling process. Parnell (1994) raises the question: "Should schools, especially public schools, be primarily in the business of instilling facts and developing so-called intellectual skills, or should they have a more practical focus as well, preparing students for the "real world" of careers . . . and the like?" (p. 37). As Alfred North Whitehead said in 1929, "But if education is not useful, what is it for?" (p. 3). Educators need to contemplate such questions related to the purpose of the educational process.

Again, the argument is back to the debate between a practical education and theory-based academic learning. The answer to this debate is not an either/or response. As we examine the technological changes in the real world, we know the answer is a combination of both. Preparing anyone today for a skilled job in the new American work force will require not only technical but academic preparation as well because of the educational requirements now demanded by most jobs. The best solution is to provide an education that connects information and knowledge with real-life experiences. As Parnell (1994) put it, "Young people of today and tomorrow need an application-rich as well as an information-rich educational program . . . education must be more than telling. It must provide opportunities for students to experience and cope with real situations—to be able to apply knowledge and to feel a sense of responsibility for their own actions" (p. 40).

We do not suggest that schools are totally to blame for the discipline and youth violence presently taking place because we know it is a much larger societal issue. It is interesting, however, and worth pondering the potential relationship that may exist between the schooling environment and accepting responsibility. On the one hand, how much have we thought about this question: *"Does a schooling environment that has relevance, direction, focus, and meaning from the student's perspective nurture responsibility?"* On the other hand, *"Does the schooling environment that tends to lack relevance, focus, and meaning from a student's perspective nurture irresponsibility?"*

Helping students understand the connection between education and their future life with meaningful, relevant learning paths can provide students with self-esteem-building experiences, enabling them to become responsible, independent, contributing citizens. As the purpose and new paradigm for education is reinvented, experience-rich learning connected to the real world must be made the highest priority.

Career Majors for All–Are We Ready?

When talking about an educational system that prepares individuals for employment, the hackles rise immediately for those who vehemently oppose utilitarian education. However, they do not become upset with colleges of medicine, law schools, engineering colleges, and aviation schools. They obviously want well-educated and skillfully trained medical doctors who keep them healthy, lawyers who can legally represent them, engineers who can build safe buildings, and pilots who can fly safely. We further surmise they are probably not opposed to good educational programs that produce academically and skillfully prepared aviation mechanics and air traffic controllers. We suspect that such Platonic classicists do not oppose preparing dentists and dental technicians, nurses and emergency medical technicians, or, for that matter, police and firefighters. Upon re-examination, we are not sure for whom the classicists oppose using educational tax dollars except for the carpenters, plumbers, electricians, welders, and machinists. This discriminating process leads to education narrowly focused on only certain careers when the elite classicist with a bachelor's degree in philosophy or history is having difficulty finding employment.

We paint this somewhat cynical scenario because of the critical times that education is now facing. Large numbers of educators and policy makers still hold the view that it is not the purpose of education to prepare our youth for jobs; yet they continue to support, through tax dollars, colleges of medicine, law, and engineering. In addition, an increasing number of parents are raising questions about spending $40,000 or more for their son's or daughter's college education that results in minimal job prospects. It does seem that reality is starting to set in as these parents question the value of their investment.

It is increasingly obvious that times are changing. Several points argue for an educational system that does a better job of preparing individuals for their future lives:

1) Business and industry want individuals who are academically and technically prepared and can apply what they have learned.

2) An increasing number of students see little relevancy in the schooling process even at the university level.

3) Parents are starting to question what they are paying for and why their children, even those who graduate from college, cannot get jobs.

4) There continues to be a shortage of highly skilled people ready to join the work force.

Goal 3 of the "Goals 2000: Educate America Act" states, "By the year 2000 . . . every school in America will ensure that all students be prepared for . . . *further learning* and *productive employment* in our modern economy" (103rd Congress, 1994, p. 3). It is quite reasonable that the central purpose of our educational process should be to prepare everyone for further learning and productive employment. Is there any young person today who does not need to be prepared for both as we approach the next century?

The importance of preparing everyone to be productive is further emphasized in goal 6 that states, "[B]y the year 2000 every adult . . . will possess the knowledge and skills necessary to compete in a global economy . . . have the opportunity to acquire the knowledge and skills, from basic to highly technical, needed to adapt to emerging new technologies, work methods and markets through public and private educational . . . programs . . ." (p. 5). Goal 6 has powerful implications for the American educational process. The primary means we have to ensure that every future adult has the knowledge and skill necessary to compete in the workplace is to have an educational system that makes such preparation its highest priority. This preparation is further supported by the passing of the landmark School-to-Work Opportunities Act of 1994 (STWOA).

STWOA strongly emphasizes the importance of all students having a career major that begins at least by the eleventh grade and is based on the individual's career interests. The act includes (103rd Congress, 1994, pp. 5–6):

- ". . . for all students to participate in high-quality, work-based learning . . . To help all students attain high academic and occupational standards . . ."

- and ". . . to expose students to a broad array of career opportunities and facilitate the selection of career majors, based on individual interests, goals, strengths, and abilities. . . ."

STWOA further defines *career major* to mean the following:

[A] coherent sequence of courses or field of study that . . . integrates academic and occupational learning, integrates school-based and work-based learning and establishes linkages between secondary schools and postsecondary institutions . . . prepares the student for employment in a broad occupational cluster . . . includes at least 2 years of secondary education and at least 1 or 2 years of postsecondary education . . . and . . . may lead to admission to a 2 or 4 year college or university. (pp. 8–9)

It is extremely important to recognize that we are talking about a career major for *all* students, not just those who are not going to college. STWOA defines *all students* to include a broad range of backgrounds including disadvantaged and academically talented students.

It is crucial that the career major be structured within a career cluster pathway that integrates the academic and occupational learning necessary for success in the area of career interest. Career clusters should be articulated and linked between secondary and postsecondary institutions, including universities, when the careers chosen require a baccalaureate or above.

Career Clusters

Developing career majors for all high school students that begin in at least the eleventh grade requires that career cluster pathways of learning be provided. The trend in many states is to provide broad career cluster pathways through which the career majors are achieved. A career cluster is defined as follows:

> A seamless program of study or career learning path that includes a broad scope or cluster of related careers in a broad field, e.g., the health and human service cluster. The career cluster pathway must include the academic as well as the technical discipline or content areas that relate to the various careers represented in the cluster. It is imperative, also, that the cluster include all careers relating to the cluster whether the career does or does not require a college or university degree.

As Kazis (1993) suggested, the clusters represent building blocks of a broad, diverse set of career pathways for young people wanting to explore and enter different industries/occupations and specialties and that the system not foreclose the possibility of higher education. Many states are using four to six clusters, grouping the various related careers into more or less the following categories or clusters:

- Business and marketing careers
- Health and human service careers
- Engineering/trade and technical careers
- Fine arts/media careers

Importantly, the clusters must be broad enough to encompass the full scope of related careers representing the complete career field and include skilled technicians as well as professional positions.

Terminating the Dual Track System

The career major/career cluster concept is an opportunity to terminate the dual tracking system. One of the most destructive aspects of the current educational system has been the perpetuation of a mind-set that suggests there is one kind of education for those who are going to college and another kind for the rest. We must terminate the mentality of "career prep" versus "college prep."

It is time to stop sorting on academic ability and to develop, instead, a success-oriented educational system around career interests and directions. By building broad career clusters and assuring that university and nonuniversity-driven careers are within the career clusters, elitist tracking is eliminated. This also assures that students are less likely to choose the college path in the absence of information about other options. We are suggesting, for example, that the future physician, as well as the future emergency medical technician and licensed practical nurse, be in the same health career cluster pathway. Likewise the future engineer would be in the engineering and industrial technology cluster along with the future electrician and machinist. The career cluster pathway would continue from high school and on to postsecondary learning through community and technical colleges as well as the universities for those students who are pursuing careers that require college and university preparation. Having broad career clusters eliminates the separate college prep track. It also helps all young people recognize that education must be goal oriented in this work-oriented society and the schooling process is related to the real world.

All Learning Is Ultimately Goal Oriented

Perhaps it is time to stop letting young people avoid choosing a direction by perpetuating a general education track that leads to nothing. In a work-oriented society, people work to live and, therefore, must choose a career path. By requiring all young people to select a career major, there will be direction, meaning, and purpose to their learning. If the cluster learning paths are designed correctly, young people changing their minds in career direction should be able to move back and forth across career majors. Because we must provide sufficient academic preparation for all future workers, the academic preparation will cut across career cluster lines. It is, however, reasonable to assume that since not all students are preparing to be high-level engineers, physicists, or mathematicians, the math and science levels should align with the performance levels required by the career major. Students will be more willing to learn academic content when it is taught in an applied contextual manner and they realize the content is required and useful to succeed in a specific career. This does, however, suggest that educators will need to establish academic performance levels in line with the real world.

Learning built around career majors and career clusters would also require that curriculum be based on broad knowledge and skill requirements. Career pathways would then incorporate the broad "workplace know-how" competencies and foundation skills that effective workers now need to know. These workplace know-how skills and knowledge areas are discussed in Chapter 7, which discusses curriculum development.

Although it is a major and radical shift in the educational paradigm, if the United States wants to remain globally competitive, we must now move to an educational system that is positively linked with the real world and prepares everyone for productive employment. Figure 6.2 depicts the career development continuum from kindergarten to employment.

CAREER DEVELOPMENT CONTINUUM

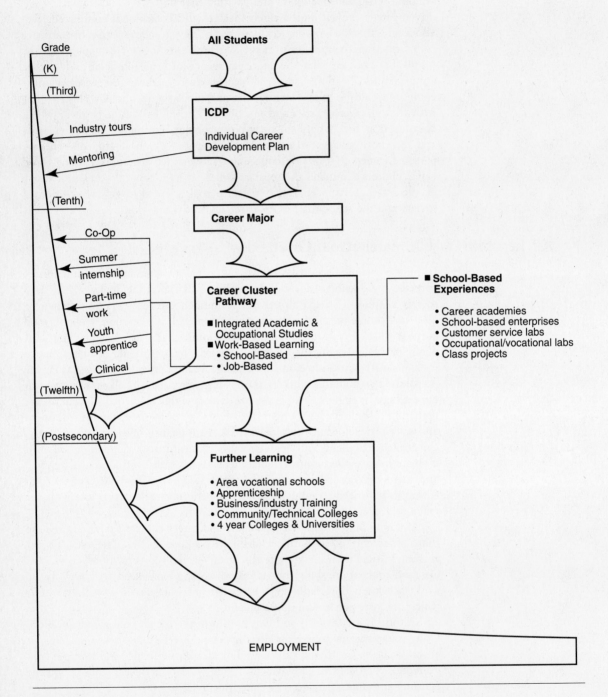

Figure 6.2
Career Development Continuum

Summary

The work force in America has gone from approximately two thirds of its workers in 1950 being unskilled to the need for approximately two thirds of its workers being skilled by the year 2000. We believe this drastic change has dramatic impact on how we reform the schooling process in the United States to align with students' present and future needs in the world of work.

The purpose of the educational system must change. No longer do we need only 20% of our high school graduates to have a good education and fill positions to organize and manage the other 80% who are less educated. It is clear we need an educational system which will provide everyone with a good education that includes the technical knowledge and skills to be successful in the new work force of the twenty-first century. Those who tend to support a classicist educational system, with little connection to the real world, must now reexamine and rethink the kind of educational system needed for the future. The work-based learning system we are prescribing will be a radical change for many.

We have reached the time when every person must develop a career and be a productive individual. Every young person must ultimately have a career major. Our school systems must provide career cluster pathways in which *all* students with adequate career counseling and Individual Career Development Plans prepare themselves for their futures. This means applied contextual learning for all students. Richard Murnane, an economist at Harvard Graduate School of Education, said, "An awful lot of kids learn skills when taught in the context of a curriculum that is related to a job rather than in the usual algebra problem that is totally unconnected to their lives" (Mathews, 1994, p. H1). We believe it is time to provide career majors for all so they see the connections to their futures.

We now have a window of opportunity to build connections between school and work through work-based learning and career majors for all *students regardless of career choice.*

References

Brustein, M. & Mahler, M. (1994). *AVA Guide to the School-to-Work Opportunities Act.* Alexandria, VA: American Vocational Association.

Caine, R. & Caine, G. (1991). *Making Connections: Teaching and the Human Brain.* Alexandria, VA: Association for Supervision and Curriculum Development.

Commission on the Skills of the American Workforce. (1990, June). *America's Choice: High Skills or Low Wages.* Rochester, NY: National Center on Education and the Economy.

103rd Congress. (1994, March). Goals 2000: Educate America Act 1994, sec. 4. H.R. 1804.

103rd Congress. (1994, May). School-to-Work Opportunities Act of 1994, sec. 3. H.R. 2884.

Kazis, R. (1993). *Improving the Transition from School to Work in the United States*. Washington, DC: American Youth Policy Forum, Competitiveness Policy Council, and Jobs for the Future.

Marshall, R., & Tucker, M. (1992). *Thinking for a Living: Education and the Wealth of Nations*. New York: Basic.

Mathews, J. (1994, March 13). "Teaching Tomorrow's Work Force." *Washington Post*, p. H1.

Parnell, D. (1994). *LogoLearning: Searching for Meaning in Education*. Waco, TX: Center for Occupational Research and Development, Inc.

Reich, R. (1992). *The Work of Nations*. New York: Vintage.

Secretary's Commission on Achieving Necessary Skills. (1991, June). *What Work Requires of Schools: A SCANS Report for America 2000*. Washington, DC: U.S. Department of Labor.

Thurow, L. (1993). *Head to Head*. New York: Morrow.

Whitehead, A. (1929). *The Aims of Education and Other Essays*. New York: Macmillan.

Chapter 7

Curriculum Development for Work-Based Learning

"Real intelligence is a creative use of knowledge, not merely an accumulation of facts. The slow thinker who can finally come up with an idea of his own is more important to the world than a walking encyclopedia who hasn't learned how to use information productively."
(Winebrenner, 1984)

The development of curriculum is one of the first steps in implementing the philosophy of a school system. Curricula at most schools are content based with little integration of course work and must be redesigned in order for work-based learning to succeed. Jacobs's (1989) statement summarized the curriculum in many schools very well: "Only in school do we have 43 minutes of math and 43 minutes of English and 43 minutes of science. Outside of school, we deal with problems and concerns in a flow of time that is not divided into knowledge fields" (p. 4).

Teachers will be expected to be knowledgeable about their discipline as well as know a broad scope of applications to the real world. This will be expensive in terms of dollars and time. Teachers will need to work with other teachers at both the secondary and postsecondary levels as well as industry personnel. Due to time constraints, much of this interaction will occur in the summer during which time teachers will have to be paid extra.

The School-to-Work Opportunities Act of 1994 (STWOA) tends to emphasize definition one from Chapter 2 and does not go far enough in stressing the point that our whole educational system needs to be overhauled to reflect a greater connection between school and work for all students. Despite this, many of the suggestions in the act for curriculum development are excellent; therefore, we feel it is worthwhile to examine them in more detail.

STWOA contains numerous directives that impact curriculum development. We concentrate on four of the areas discussed: (1) integrating academic and occupational learning, (2) integrating school-based and work-based learning; (3) establishing linkages between secondary schools and postsecondary educational institutions; and (4) developing a school system that leads to further education and training. In addition to these four areas, the following are examined:

(5) curriculum development and the SCANS report, *What Work Requires of Schools*; (6) assessment; and (7) steps in curriculum development.

Integrating Academic and Occupational Learning

Integrating academic and occupational learning is at the core of most, if not all, of the school-to-work initiative and is given in the STWOA as one of the three levels of integration. As the quote by Jacobs cited in the first paragraph implies, schools often divide disciplines whereas in life, knowledge is integrated. Teachers have been and still are expected to teach a subject focusing narrowly on content with little emphasis on how that content relates to other subject matter or the real world.

Unfortunately, our educational system distinguishes between academic and occupational courses. This distinction has even greater impact when students are labeled college bound or non-college bound. It is our hope that someday the lines will become so blurred that the terms *academic* and *occupational* will no longer be used. Simply, the vision is for all courses to be academically rigorous and contain occupational, work-oriented applications of the content. After all, one of the greatest benefits of work-based learning is that it helps students learn academic material by showing relevancy.

Integration of academic and occupational learning should occur in all courses throughout the schooling process, emphasizing definition two of work-based learning. To quote from definition two, "from the beginning of schooling" and "a theme or focus that people work in order to live": That is, integration of academic and occupational learning must be systemic for the entire educational process.

The decision to integrate content is often seen as a yes or no decision; however, there are shades of gray. Jacobs (1989) lists a continuum of options for content design along with examples of each:

1) **Discipline Based:** This is the traditional design and format of education where separate subjects are taught in separate time blocks. In this model, no integration is attempted. Examples of the discipline-based design are prevalent in schools today. Algebra, history, and English are just a few of the subjects commonly taught in this manner. Subjects are presented without an attempt to show the relationship among them. As the schooling process is reformed, we hope this model will receive less emphasis.

2) **Parallel Disciplines:** In this design option, teachers sequence their content to mesh with lessons in other classrooms. Content does not change, but rather, the order in which content is presented changes so related topics are discussed at similar times in different courses. It is important to note that teachers do not actively pursue linking content across subject areas. The courses are simply resequenced with the hope that students will make the links among subject matter. An example Jacobs provided was that of a social studies class studying a World War II unit in the

beginning of the spring semester and the English teacher rescheduling her autumn semester book, *Summer of My German Soldier,* to coincide with the World War II lesson. Teachers must communicate with each other, but not adapt the content—just reshuffle when content is presented.

3) *Complementary Disciplinary Units/Courses:* This option brings together related disciplines to form a formal unit or course to investigate a theme or issue. Even disciplines that do not appear to be related can be brought together under this method as long as the disciplines complement each other in the issue being explored. For example, a course called "Ethics in Science" combines the disciplines of ethics and science.

4) *Interdisciplinary Units/Courses:* In this option, a full range of disciplines is brought together under one course or unit. The course or unit is designed to coexist with the discipline-based approach. A business strategy (also called business policy) course offered in many colleges of business is a good example. Business students usually enroll in this type of course during their last semester before graduation. Case analysis is the primary instructional method. The course is designed so students apply all their knowledge with emphasis on their business courses in marketing, management, finance, and accounting. However, all course material can be integrated into cases because there will be other important issues, including ethical (philosophy), environmental (science), governmental (political science), cultural (history, religion), and logistical (geography). This example also hints at the importance of the academic or liberal arts courses and shows that these courses can be connected to students' future lives.

5) *Integrated Day:* This approach focuses on the students' questions and interests rather than a predetermined content. This method is commonly seen in preschools and kindergarten. Time is structured around the needs of the student and content is adapted accordingly. This method has little chance of success at the higher grade levels because there is no guarantee that core requirements will ever be met.

6) *Complete Program:* This option is perhaps the most interesting form of interdisciplinary work and totally integrates the student's life with school. The lives of the students are the driving theme or focus for the school. Students live in the school environment and create the curriculum from their daily living. Students interested in buildings on campus might study architecture. If there is a conflict between students and administration at the school, students might study government. Again, with this approach, there is no guarantee that the core material would receive attention. A. S. Neill's Summerhill is an example of this design where students do not learn a specific subject until they are ready and interested in learning.

For the adventurous teacher, the last two alternatives appear especially interesting. These options attempt to tap into students' natural curiosity. However, with various state and local standards, they will be difficult to implement. Gardner (1983) hypothesized seven forms of intelligence: linguistic, logical/mathematical, musical, spatial, kinesthetic, interpersonal, and intrapersonal. Although it is beyond the scope of this discussion to review each form of intelligence, it is important to know that everyone has some ability in each; however, the level varies from person to person. If one believes Gardner's hypothesis and that tapping into students' natural curiosity is wise, a strong argument for a flexible curriculum with student participation can be made.

Theorists have proposed applying empowerment management principles in the classroom, which suggests that students should have more say in what they learn and how they are taught. Many of these principles are designed to seek information about what students want to learn and how they learn with the goal of increasing their motivation and tapping into their personal learning styles. There is much to consider when proposing the use of business principles in the classroom. Modern management theory suggests that managers should empower workers by letting them participate in decision making, goal setting, and so on. This can be applied to education. Asking students to be participants in what is to be taught and how it should be taught can both empower and motivate them. Modern marketing theory suggests that it is wise to find out what the customer wants and then fill that need. If we treat our students as customers, it only makes sense to seek information on how to best meet their needs. The point in this discussion is that curriculum development and classroom management should not leave the students out. The students' input can be extremely useful. This is especially true in designing work-based curricula that relates to their futures as productive individuals.

Many methods for integrating vocational and academic education have gained widespread attention. In addition to the eight models described in Figure 7.1, the work-based strategies discussed in Chapter 4 are methods of integrating academic and occupational material. All of these models and strategies concentrate on the high school and postsecondary levels. Many of them emphasize integrating math, science, and English courses with occupational courses. This is a good start; however, it is only the beginning. Throughout this book we emphasize that schools and work need to have greater connectedness. Although we are fully supportive of the continuing experimentation with all these strategies and models, it is clear the emphasis within all strategies and models align with definition one (Chapter 2) of work-based learning.

We realize patience is needed and change cannot happen overnight. Regardless, there is a fear that these strategies and methods will be viewed as an upgrade to vocational education. This is the danger in emphasizing definition one.

We must go beyond definition one and concentrate on definition two of work-based learning. The schooling process must not only include work-based programs that concentrate on hands-on experiences. People work to live and there must be a positive connectedness for all students between education and living productive lives. We must be careful not to settle for a curriculum that is simply a tweaking of the current system. While waiting for the educational

Model 1: Incorporating Academic Competencies Into Vocational Courses

a) Probably simplest form of integration.

b) Relabeling of the informal reinforcement of basic academic skills in vocational classes.

c) Using developed off-the-shelf curriculum materials which identify academic competencies.

d) Academic competencies stressed are generally simple or lower level.

e) Does nothing to change the separation between academic and vocational teachers, programs, and students.

f) Taught by vocational teachers.

Model 2: Combining Academic and Vocational Teachers

a) Academic teachers initiate the teaching of academic competencies in vocational programs.

b) Assigning academic teachers to Area Vocational Center part- or full-time to work with vocational teacher or team teaching.

c) Strength of this model is in collaboration.

d) Presence of academic teacher gives status to academic skills.

e) Most academic content is remedial.

Model 3: Making Academic Curriculum More Vocationally Relevant

a) Academic teachers incorporate vocational examples into their courses.

b) More common approach is to introduce specific new courses "applied academics."

c) Sometimes used to substitute for lower level academic courses.

d) Used as electives with no courses dropped from the course offerings.

e) Most popular form of integration.

f) Unless linked to vocational programs and teachers, true integration may not take place.

Model 4: Modifying Academic and Vocational Education—Curriculum "Alignment"

a) Changes the content of both academic and vocational courses.

b) Coordinates existing teachers and courses.

c) Relies on locally developed curricula.

d) Incorporates elements from Models 2 and 3.

e) Many teachers use Applied Academic materials.

f) Teacher collaboration and student mixing.

g) Cooperative learning.

Model 5: Academy Model

a) Operate as schools within schools.

b) Teacher collaboration.

c) Student groups work with teacher groups.

d) Business, industry relationships.

e) Motivate potential dropouts.

f) Does not reduce tracking of students.

Model 6: Replacing Conventional Departments with Occupational Clusters

a) Replace conventional departments.

b) Departments organized along occupational lines.

c) Career-cluster department recommends specific course sequence.

d) Promotes teacher collaboration.

e) Reduces "turfism."

f) Expanded Academy Model.

g) Reduces tracking of students.

Model 7: Single-Occupation High Schools

a) Similar to academies except occupational emphasis is school-wide.

b) Academic instruction is more vocational.

c) Reduces student tracking.

d) Promotes opportunities for teacher collaboration.

Model 8: Electing Career Paths or Occupational Majors

a) Maintain conventional academic and vocational departments.

b) Students elect a "career path" to follow.

c) Integrate career-related information into academic subjects.

d) Reduces "curriculum cafeteria" approach.

Figure 7.1 Models of Integration (*Source: Law, D. A., & Pepple, J. D. (1990, November).*)

paradigm to shift to a greater emphasis on learning that relates to being productive, educators must move forward in developing work-based learning curricula.

Integrating School-Based and Work-Based Learning

Because of the different definitions of work-based learning, integration of school-based and work-based learning can have different interpretations. Chapter 2 discussed two definitions of work-based learning. STWOA does not explicitly define the term *work-based learning*, but there is an implicit definition. We believe the School-to-Work Opportunities Act of 1994 uses the term to mean job-based or site-based learning. That is, work-based learning in the STWOA is equivalent to the terms *job-based* or *site-based learning* used in this book. We continue to use these terms to mean learning that, for the most part, occurs at a business or industry location.

Ideally, school-based learning should integrate work-based learning and vice versa. Learning on school premises, typically in the classroom, should attempt to integrate the applications students are using in their job-based experiences. Likewise, work-based experiences should apply information learned in the classroom.

Job-based learning integrated into school-based learning requires that teachers have a good understanding of what students are learning in their job-based experiences. Academic teachers can visit local businesses to obtain an understanding of both the businesses and the experiences students will encounter. However, teachers should not be afraid to learn from their students. Teachers do not need to know all the answers; in fact, it is impossible. Teachers can gain an understanding of how their subject area is applied in the world of work through the experiences of their students. In many locations, students will be at a variety of job sites, making it difficult for teachers to communicate with so many industry personnel. Because most students will not have job-based experiences, at least in the early phases of implementation for work-based learning, teachers will have to be flexible. The classroom may consist of students working at a variety of job-based locations along with students who have no job-based experiences. This diversity can enhance the classroom and help all students and teachers learn a broad array of applications for content.

School-based learning integrated into job-based activities is also a challenge. With the need for these job-based experiences to be tools for teaching academic content, there is an implied responsibility for business and industry personnel to understand and know what students are learning in the classroom.

For integration to occur the way STWOA is intended, a structured and well-defined communication process between teachers and industry personnel is imperative. Making the process effective and efficient could prove to be a great challenge.

Establishing Linkages Between Secondary Schools and Postsecondary Educational Institutions

A second level of integration called for in STWOA is integration of secondary and post-secondary learning (103 Congress, 1994). Such linking secondary and postsecondary curriculum (articulation) also implies effective communication between secondary and postsecondary educators. Curriculum development becomes a multischool process rather than a school-by-school process. This is already occurring in some of the Tech Prep programs.

It is clear the task for educators is huge. Implementing work-based concepts requires a well-organized plan that supports teachers. Curriculum materials can be a major support; the lack of appropriate materials can result in failure. To expect high school teachers to meet with occupational teachers, postsecondary teachers, and business and industry representatives while continuing to be responsible for all their other activities is asking the impossible. Thus part of the solution is to have teacher involvement with curriculum development occur primarily during the summer as part of professional development. This shift from content-based learning to articulated, integrated work-based learning will require financial support for the team that is writing curriculum during the summer.

Developing a School System That Leads to Further Education and Training

The options for students must remain open if tracking is eliminated. Students should be obtaining the academic skills necessary to pursue further learning when it is appropriate. Work-based learning is not a watered-down curriculum that minimizes further learning options.

The other side of the coin rarely emphasized is the traditionally labeled college-bound student. STWOA includes "academically talented students" in the definition of *all students*. That is, school-to-work opportunities are not just for the forgotten half, neglected majority, non-college bound, and so on. School-to-work opportunities are to benefit all students. The advantages of work-based learning, from a learner's standpoint, include making learning more meaningful.

As alluded to earlier, cognitive psychology suggests that people learn best when new information can be integrated with what they know. Teaching in a hands-on, applied manner can help all students learn more effectively. By tying new information into their knowledge structures, students can learn more efficiently. Concrete examples are important. Abstract knowledge is much more difficult to tie to one's past knowledge (knowledge structure) thereby making it difficult to grasp new concepts. Likewise, rote memorization is also difficult due to the difficulty of relating the information to other past concepts that have been learned. Most educators know this about learning, however, the gap between that knowledge and some current teaching methods still in use remains. Part of the problem is that teachers are working with outdated curriculum materials. The curriculum clearly needs to be reshaped to conform to a more contextual style.

Hull (1993) has an excellent chapter on contextual learning:

> According to contextual learning theory, learning occurs only when students (learners) process new information or knowledge in such a way that it makes sense to them in their frame of reference (their own inner world of memory, experience, and response). This approach to learning and teaching assumes that the mind naturally seeks meaning in context—that is, in the environment where the person is located—and that it does so through searching for relationships that make sense and appear

useful . . . students discover meaningful relationships between abstract ideas and practical applications in the context of the real world, and concepts are internalized through the process of discovering, reinforcing, and interrelating these relationships (p. 41).

Simply, most people learn better in hands-on application-oriented learning environments. When new material is presented by relating it to current knowledge, the new concepts are more likely to be learned. Teaching in an abstract way without application is not consistent with what cognitive psychologists are telling us. To be sure, the majority of the abstract thinkers are the college-bound students. It does not make sense to teach in only one way, especially when that one way caters to the 80th percentile and above (by traditional measurement standards), unless we want to continue using our schools as sorting devices rather than preparing people for life.

What Work Requires of Schools

Although specific skills vary from job to job, the report *What Work Requires of Schools: A SCANS Report for America 2000* (1991) established "workplace know-how" components consisting of five competencies and a three-part foundation of skills and personal qualities that are needed for solid job performance (Figures 7.2 and 7.3). These competencies and skills can serve as the foundation for developing curriculum.

It is very difficult to argue against the importance of these various competencies and personal qualities regardless of the students' career direction. It is, therefore, imperative to factor them into developing the curriculum. With these various competencies and qualities woven into our educational system, the classroom is likely to be a much different place. Figure 7.4 compares the conventional classroom to what a SCANS classroom would be like.

As can be seen by this comparison, a SCANS classroom requires a new way of teaching. Although many of the course titles may not change, what is actually occurring in the classroom will be quite different if the SCANS classroom becomes a reality. In addition, with many work-based learning strategies, the classroom will be "without walls"; many of the activities will be done outside the classroom. This educational system will demand new and innovative curriculum materials. Such materials will need to be applied and contextual in nature and relate to workplace know-how skills.

Assessment

A major overhaul is also needed in our assessment techniques. We cannot shift to a work-based learning mode and still assess students using paper-and-pencil tests that quiz students on memorization and mere regurgitation of facts.

Educators are developing a variety of alternative assessment methods. The National Center for Research in Vocational Education teleconference *Assessment 2000: An Exhibition* (1993) provided excellent information on alternative

Resources: Identifies, Organizes, Plans, and Allocates Resources

A) *Time*—selects goal-relevant activities, ranks them, allocates time, and prepares and follows schedules

B) *Money*—uses or prepares budgets, makes forecasts, keeps records, and makes adjustments to meet objectives

C) *Material and Facilities*—acquires, stores, allocates, and uses materials or space efficiently

D) *Human Resources*—assesses skills and distributes work accordingly; evaluates performance, and provides feedback

Interpersonal: Works with Others

A) *Participates as Member of a Team*—contributes to group effort

B) *Teaches Others New Skills*

C) *Serves Clients/Customers*—works to satisfy customers' expectations

D) *Exercises Leadership*—communicates ideas to justify position, persuades and convinces others, responsibly challenges existing procedures and policies

E) *Negotiates*—works toward agreements involving exchange of resources, resolves divergent interests

F) *Works with Diversity*—works well with men and women from diverse backgrounds

Information: Acquires and Uses Information

A) *Acquires and Evaluates Information*

B) *Organizes and Maintains Information*

C) *Interprets and Communicates Information*

D) *Uses Computers to Process Information*

Systems: Understands Complex Interrelationships

A) *Understands Systems*—knows how social, organizational, and technological systems work and operates effectively with them

B) *Monitors and Corrects Performance*—distinguishes trends, predicts impacts on system operations, diagnoses deviations in systems' performance, and corrects malfunctions

C) *Improves or Designs Systems*—suggests modifications to existing systems and develops new or alternative systems to improve performance

Technology: Works with a Variety of Technologies

A) *Selects Technology*—chooses procedures, tools, or equipment including computers and related technologies

B) *Applies Technology to Task*—understands overall intent and proper procedures for setup and operation of equipment

C) *Maintains and Troubleshoots Equipment*—prevents, identifies, or solves problems with equipment, including computers and other technologies

Figure 7.2 Five Competencies *(Source: Secretary's Commission on Achieving Necessary Skills. (1991).)*

assessment methods. The three assessment methods focused on were *student projects, performance event,* and *portfolio*. The student project usually entails the development of a physical product. The performance event involves a demonstration applying knowledge or skills to a real or simulated work situation. The portfolio is a comprehensive collection of a student's work that demonstrates his or her skills, knowledge, and abilities. How these various projects take shape is limited only by the restrictions that students and teachers put in their minds.

Basic Skills: Reads, Writes, Performs Arithmetic and Mathematical Operations, Listens, and Speaks

A) *Reading*—locates, understands, and interprets written information in prose and in documents such as manuals, graphs, and schedules

B) *Writing*—communicates thoughts, ideas, information, and messages in writing; and creates documents such as letters, directions, manuals, reports, graphs, and flow charts

C) *Arithmetic/Mathematics*—performs basic computations and approaches practical problems by choosing appropriately from a variety of mathematical techniques

D) *Listening*—receives, attends to, interprets, and responds to verbal messages and other cues

E) *Speaking*—organizes ideas and communicates orally

Thinking Skills: Thinks Creatively, Makes Decisions, Solves Problems, Visualizes, Knows How to Learn, and Reasons

A) *Creative Thinking*—generates new ideas

B) *Decision Making*—specifies goals and constraints, generates alternatives, considers risks, and evaluates and chooses best alternative

C) *Problem Solving*—recognizes problems and devises and implements plan of action

D) *Seeing Things in the Mind's Eye*—organizes and processes symbols, pictures, graphs, objects, and other information

E) *Knowing How to Learn*—uses efficient learning techniques to acquire and apply new knowledge and skills

F) *Reasoning*—discovers a rule or principle underlying the relationship between two or more objects and applies it in solving a problem

Personal Qualities: Displays Responsibility, Self-Esteem, Sociability, Self-Management, and Integrity and Honesty

A) *Responsibility*—exerts a high level of effort and perseveres toward goal attainment

B) *Self-Esteem*—believes in own self-worth and maintains a positive view of self

C) *Sociability*—demonstrates understanding, friendliness, adaptability, empathy, and politeness in group settings

D) *Self-Management*—assesses self accurately, sets personal goals, monitors progress, and exhibits self-control

E) *Integrity/Honesty*—chooses ethical courses of action

Figure 7.3 A Three-Part Foundation *(Source: Secretary's Commission on Achieving Necessary Skills. (1991).)*

These alternative assessment methods provide for some exciting opportunities to make educational assessment more consistent with what the student will face in life and more relevant to what they have actually learned and are able to apply.

Assessment should help orchestrate curriculum design. If the assessment techniques are valid and worthwhile, curriculum is designed around the assessment standards. It is wiser to first formulate assessment philosophies and methods and structure the curriculum around assessment than vice versa. So often teachers are forced to teach to the test. This is not bad if the test, the form of assessment, is appropriate.

One of the secrets to good teaching is good testing. At first glance, this

From the Conventional Classroom	To the SCANS Classroom
Teacher knows answer.	More than one solution may be viable and teacher may not have it in advance.
Students routinely work alone.	Students routinely work with teachers, peers, and community members.
Teacher plans all activities.	Students and teachers plan and negotiate activities.
Teacher decides method of assessment. Information is organized, evaluated, interpreted, and communicated to students by teachers.	Students routinely assess themselves. Information is acquired, evaluated, organized, interpreted, and communicated by students to appropriate audiences.
Organization system of the classroom is simple: One teacher teaches 30 students.	Organizing systems are complex: Teacher and students agree on organization and reach out beyond school for traditional information.
Reading, writing, and math are treated as separate disciplines; listening and speaking often are missing from curriculum.	Knowledge needed for problem solving is integrated; listening and speaking are fundamental parts of learning.
Thinking is usually theoretical and "academic."	Thinking involves problem solving, reasoning, and decision making.
Students are expected to conform to teacher's behavioral expectations; integrity and honesty are monitored by teacher; student self-esteem is often poor.	Students are expected to be responsible, sociable, self-managing, and resourceful; integrity and honesty are monitored within the social context of the classroom; students' self-esteem is high because they are in charge of their own learning.

Figure 7.4   The Conventional Classroom and the SCANS Classroom *(Source: "Move to Create High-Performance Schools," (1992, May 11), p. 4.)*

statement appears to be controversial. However, this statement is instrumental in developing a work-based curriculum as long as teachers teach to the test and the test is an excellent measure of what students need to know.

Presently, there is little relationship to performance in the classroom and whether the student will succeed in the work world. There simply are not many multiple-choice tests in the world of work. If assessment methods in schools can match what is expected in life, teaching to help the particular assessment method makes sense. Figure 7.5 provides a schematic of this concept. In mathematical terms, if $A = B$ and $B = C$, then $A = C$. A is curriculum; B is assessment; C is life and work. If students can successfully accomplish B (assessment), they should be successful in work and life; the curriculum is teaching the appropriate material. That is, B must match C. It then makes sense to teach to the test (align A and B). Unfortunately, our current system breaks down because student

Figure 7.5

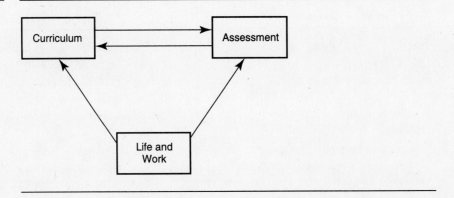

performance and assessment methods do not always match, nor are they consistent with the world of work and life. There is not a strong relationship between B (assessment) and C (life and work) or A (curriculum) and C. Simply stated, there is too much disconnectedness between our schools and life.

The issue we are raising in this discussion implies that assessment strategies must be revisited and intensively reviewed throughout the total schooling process from kindergarten through postgraduate work. The key to good assessment is the relationship of the assessment to the expected outcomes of the learning experiences.

Another way to look at assessment is to review the medical model of assessment in the health-care industry where its primary purpose is to determine diagnostically the current state of health in relation to the preferred state of health. Figure 7.6 (I) graphically illustrates how the medical model functions to move the patient via the cycle of diagnosis, prescribed treatment, diagnosis,

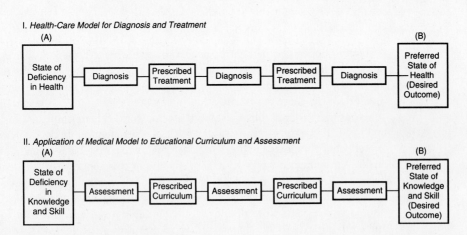

Figure 7.6

prescribed treatment until the preferred state of health is reached. This model, however, is predicated on several basic premises: First, the current state of health is measurable and recognized as a deficiency by the patient; second, the preferred outcomes are known and desired by both the patient (client) and the practitioner; and third, change and improvement will more than likely result if the right treatment is provided in a way best for the individual or patient.

Applying the Medical Model to Education

The application of the medical model to educational curriculum and assessment, as in the health setting, is predicated also on the same basic premises: First, the current state of knowledge and skill is measurable and recognized as a deficiency by the learner; second, the preferred outcomes are known and desired by both the learner (client) and the teacher (practitioner), and; third, change, improvement, and growth will more than likely result if the right curriculum (treatment) is provided in a way best for the individual or learner. Figure 7.6 (II) further depicts how the learner with a recognized deficiency in knowledge and skill moves via the cycle of assessment, prescribed curriculum, assessment, prescribed curriculum until the preferred state of knowledge and skill is obtained.

Although a somewhat simplistic explanation of the application of the medical model to education, we believe such a model has strong implications for education. It does almost totally require an outcome-based orientation to all of education. One could quite strongly argue that there is little reason for people to interface with the schooling process if there is no need for change on the part of the individual. Or, put in another way, the major purpose of the schooling process must be to move the learner from point (A) to (B) via assessment and clearly defined outcome-based curriculum repeated throughout the schooling process until desired outcome levels of knowledge and skill are obtained. This form of learning places the emphasis on the outcomes instead of the process. Because there is little connection in the current educational system to the real world and what the students will be able to do as a result of schooling, our present educational process is a content and process-oriented system.

We have continued to stress the importance of connections between the schooling process and what students become and are able to do as a result of such schooling. The emphasis must be on the desired outcomes, and the curriculum and assessment must be clearly linked and connected to such outcomes. The assessment process then must be primarily a diagnostic tool to determine where learners are in relationship to where they want to be. Thus assessment would not be used as a sorting device, as currently it too often is, but instead as a positive tool to help determine or select the next step of the curriculum leading to predetermined outcomes or educational goals.

College Admissions

Because so much emphasis is placed on meeting and qualifying for college admissions, it can be asked what the effects and impact of the thinking described here would be on college admissions exams and procedures. Since current college admissions processes are sorting devices based primarily on educational achievement scores, the process is not diagnostic.

As the concept of applied work-based learning expands in the secondary level and greater connections are formed between education and work, assessment throughout education will become more diagnostic. As the primary purpose of educational assessment becomes one of determining capability in relationship to some career goal, college and university admissions requirements will need to change drastically. If universities were to shift emphasis from simply a place to go to obtain a college education to a place to prepare for a career that requires university preparation, then admissions procedures would need to align with a diagnostic analysis which would determine students' current knowledge and skill as related to their career paths. The admissions process would assess whether the students had the basic knowledge and skills needed to prepare them for the given career path they wished to pursue and would require students to have a career major in mind rather than use the bachelor's degree as a career exploration method. This kind of admissions exam would then determine if they have the prerequisite knowledge and skill to enter the program. Some would view this as sorting; however, it is not sorting to keep out students, but rather to determine the entrance point of students in a program or to diagnose what needs to be studied to enroll in a program. No longer would all students begin university programs as freshmen. If they had already acquired certain skills required in their prospective career through past experiences, they would then start further along the career learning path. This requires a competency-based curriculum instead of a sequence of courses that everyone takes regardless of preexisting knowledge and skill. Continuing our previous analogy, most medical practitioners administer their treatments based on the diagnosis of the patient rather than prescribing the same treatment to all patients regardless of condition.

Again, this is a radical deviation from the traditional pattern. If, however, as a society including the education profession we can decide that education must be connected to living our lives as self-supporting productive, contributing members of society, the paradigm will change. Following this line of thinking would greatly alter the current use of assessment. The new paradigm will have curriculum paths closely aligned with career pursuits. Assessment will not be used as a sorting device but as a diagnostic tool to determine the curriculum for reaching one's career goal.

Assessment would diagnose one's abilities, what one can do, and one's current knowledge and skill in relationship to what one wants to be or do. This changes the negative connotation of assessment to that of a positive tool used for prescribing appropriate curriculum. This method of assessment will require major mind-set changes by educators who view testing and assessment as a way of sorting or categorizing students for grades and determining who gets certain opportunities and who does not. We believe moving to an educational system that is about preparing individuals to be successful in future career pursuits will require a new paradigm for educational measurement and assessment from kindergarten to postdoctoral study.

Steps in Curriculum Development

Curriculum development can be complex and time consuming. We provide a broad overview of some of the steps involved; however, we recommend using a curriculum development book to learn the intricacies of this complex process. Figure 7.7 provides 18 steps (not necessarily sequential) for developing a work-based learning curriculum.

Within this process, it is important to determine the strengths and weaknesses of the current curriculum. In fact, it is probably wise to analyze the strengths and weaknesses of the whole schooling process including business/industry involvement. Are teachers enthusiastic about work-based learning? Are there opportunities for business leaders to participate in curriculum development? What is the relationship between the school system and the business community? These are a few of the questions worth pondering.

---

1) Develop understanding and acceptance of concepts of integrated and applied work-based curriculum.
2) Determine specific career fields for which learning paths are being developed.
3) Determine program development team.
4) Determine learning outcomes to be achieved.
5) Determine whether outcomes can be accomplished in specific courses, programs, basic core, or occupational specialty courses
6) Identify integrated model or format, for example, single program, career cluster, career academy, and so on.
7) Identify business/industry work-based experiences to be incorporated in program, for example, co-op, on-the-job training, apprenticeship, internship, and so on.
8) Determine students and grade levels for program.
9) Develop curriculum outline.
10) Identify resources and curriculum materials.
11) Develop (write) curriculum.
12) Arrange curriculum in logical sequence.
13) Determine program delivery format: individual courses, team teaching, block scheduling, and so on.
14) Identify subjects, disciplines, and teachers to deliver curriculum.
15) Identify secondary and postsecondary roles.
16) Develop integrated applied instructional units.
17) Implement program.
18) Conduct program evaluation.

Figure 7.7   Developing a Work-Based Learning Curriculum

Several options are open to those ready to employ work-based curriculum materials. One option is for teachers and educators to develop them. This is more time consuming than developing content-based curriculum materials because of the knowledge of work applications required. Preparation from a single textbook will not work because textbooks, in general, do not have a work-based emphasis. A second option is to purchase curriculum materials. Although this is expensive, work-based learning can be implemented more rapidly. Teachers can devote their time to teaching rather than developing materials. However, presently, there is a shortage of work-based curriculum materials. As work-based learning evolves, textbooks and other supplies will adapt. Lastly, a hybrid approach to developing curriculum materials could be used with teachers adapting commercial materials. The advantage of this method is that it gives teachers a head start while still giving them the freedom to emphasize different areas they feel are important. Regardless of the option chosen, all courses and levels of learning must be saturated with contextual materials in order to draw connections between the schooling process and being a productive individual.

Business representatives can be instrumental in shaping curricula. Although educators should maintain the lead in curricula development because they are knowledgeable in curriculum development strategies, business leaders can provide a wealth of information and suggestions on application exercises. As the world changes, the business community can be the pulse on change for educators and, in turn, keep the curriculum up to date.

The DACUM (developing a curriculum) process is one of the most popular industry-driven methods used to develop a work-based curriculum. The DACUM process starts with experts in a career field who meet to provide information on the skills and knowledge needed in a specific career area. The first step usually develops the main categories. The panel of experts then brainstorms within each category to determine the necessary tasks and knowledge for an individual to perform in a career. During this brainstorming period, an educator records the tasks, knowledge, and other pertinent information needed to further develop the curriculum. The panel of experts may retain the information from the brainstorming period in order to provide additional input. The end result is a comprehensive list of skills and knowledge needed to be successful in a career area.

From this list, educators develop curriculum materials and course content. The panel of experts is not generally involved in determining the instructional processes. The major purpose of the business/industry experts is to provide information on careers. This process can help academic teachers understand how their course content is used; however, because some teachers may not be familiar with some of the specific terminology, it may be necessary for teachers to seek the help of either vocational teachers or people in the field to obtain a better understanding of the applications.

Number 4 of Figure 7.7, determining learning outcomes to be achieved, hints at the importance of obtaining a wide variety of support for work-based learning. Community and employer expectations, national skill standards, skill certification requirements, and state requirements must be incorporated into the process. Schools often respond to state requirements by dividing time into blocks to categorize content and to maintain responsibility. State requirements are often stated in terms of minutes per week. Jacobs (1989) stated, ". . . 8 times a day, students leap out of their seats every 40 minutes and rush for 5 minutes to another setting, another subject, another teacher, another set of students" (p. 4). This paradigm needs to change.

Summary

There are probably more questions than answers when discussing the best way to develop a work-based curriculum. Educators have endless options because experimentation is ongoing throughout the country. Integration of learning needs to mesh and eventually blur distinctions between the academic and occupational modes. The curriculum must be designed around work-based learning for *all* students. Applied, relevant, contextual learning is an effective instructional technique. *What Work Requires of Schools* provides a guide to what skills and abilities are important to consider when structuring the curriculum. Assessment that is harmonious with work-based learning is critical to avoid tracking.

It is extremely dangerous to dictate from a top-down perspective and tell teachers what to do. Teachers must feel empowered and that they have a say in their classroom. Teachers, parents and students must all be involved in the curriculum development process. We are confident that both parents and students will support work-based learning. Teachers, we expect, will have a wide range of opinions.

The curriculum must shift from content based to a curriculum that focuses on the needs of students. The needs of students focus around their future lives as productive citizens. Therefore, the curriculum must be connected to the world of work and life.

References

Assessment 2000: An Exhibition. (1993). Berkeley, CA: National Center for Research in Vocational Education.

Gardner, H. (1983). *Frames of Mind: The Theory of Multiple Intelligences.* New York: Basic Books.

Jacobs, H. (Ed.). (1989). *Interdisciplinary Curriculum: Design and Implementation.* Alexandria, VA: Association for Supervision and Curriculum.

Hull, D. (1993). *Opening Minds, Opening Doors: The Rebirth of American Education.* Waco, TX: Center for Occupational Research and Development.

Law, D., & Pepple, J. (1990, November). *Integrated Curriculum: A Nationwide Perspective and Integration Models That Are Working.* Papers presented at the Curriculum Integration in Outcome-Based System: Making the Mission Reality meeting, Greely, CO.

"Move to Create High-Performance School." (1992, May 11). *Vocational Education Weekly* 5(6), pp. 3–4.

103rd Congress. (1994, May). School-to-Work Opportunities Act of 1994, H.R. 2884.

Secretary's Commission on Achieving Necessary Skills. (1991). *What Work Requires of Schools: A SCANS Report for America 2000.* Washington, DC: U.S. Department of Labor.

Winebrenner, D. (1984). *The Forbes Scrapbook of Thoughts on the Business of Life* (vol 2). New York: Forbes, p. 377.

Chapter 8

Role of Business and Industry

"[W]e must marshal the resources that exist in our vast business infrastructures and employee organizations to join with schools in preparing young people for citizen responsibility and employment."
(Council of Chief State School Officers, 1992)

Perhaps equally as significant as the philosophical changes educators must make, discussed in Chapter 3, are the changes that business and industry leaders will have to adopt if the goals for work-based learning are to be realized. Business, industry, government, labor, and employers can all participate in changing education. The STWOA of 1994 specifically refers to the integration between school-based and work-based learning and the connecting activities that need to be developed (103rd Congress, 1994). At present the roles of these entities regarding education have, in general, not been clearly defined; thus a practical approach to getting business/industry involved needs to be developed. Businesses already support education in the form of taxes. With work-based strategies, businesses are being asked to devote even more money, as well as time. On a small experimental stage, business has been cooperating with educators. However, implementation of work-based strategies on a large scale requires a major commitment. Are our business leaders up to this commitment? What roadblocks are there to obtaining the cooperation of businesses? What will get businesses interested in participating in education? These are some of the questions we address in this chapter.

With the various work-based learning strategies outlined in Chapter 4 there are a number of ways that business and industry can become involved. Although there may be overlap, roles of business and industry can be categorized into school-based and job-based. Because the job-based strategies as discussed in Chapter 4 are limited, not all students will be involved in job-based learning. Therefore, the roles of business and industry for school-based learning are critical. School-based industry roles are primarily indirect in nature whereas the job-based roles of business and industry involve a higher degree of commitment from companies on a daily basis and intensive student participation. It can be argued that the skill level of business and industry people involved in job-based learning of students is more complex than school-based since they need a sound understanding of instructional strategies. Following are the subcategories of the school-based and job-based roles of business and industry:

School-Based Roles of Business and Industry

1) Providing in-service education for teachers
2) Participating in curriculum development
3) Providing guest speakers and business/industry tours
4) Providing equipment and supplies
5) Participating in business/school partnerships

Job-Based Roles of Business and Industry

1) Providing job-based learning experiences
2) Providing mentors and masters

School-Based Roles of Business and Industry
Providing In-Service Education for Teachers

As previously mentioned, many teachers do not know how their subject matter is applied in the work world. There are a number of ways businesses can help with in-service education for teachers: (1) offer site visits; (2) answer educators' questions; (3) provide part-time and summer employment; and (4) provide mentors for teachers.

Site visits can range from onetime experiences to periodic visits of facilities. Spending a couple of weeks in the summer visiting a variety of companies could give teachers a new outlook on how to teach. Teacher tours can be extremely beneficial in bringing awareness of what students' future work sites might entail. Site visits where industry participants spend significantly large blocks of time with teachers would provide a huge advantage to teachers in curriculum development.

Having industry representatives available to answer questions is imperative, especially in the early stages. As educators develop and implement an applied curriculum, many questions are likely to emerge. Knowing there is technical support can ease teacher anxiety when approaching new methods of teaching in an applied and work-based manner.

Teachers who are interested in experiencing the work world that many of their students will soon be facing should consider part-time or summer employment at a local business. Work-based learning encourages "learning by doing." Therefore, it makes sense for teachers to learn by participating in noneducational work experiences.

Not only do students need mentors, but so do teachers. These mentorship activities can occur during the summer and continue through the school year. The mentor may be the one who organizes the site visits, answers questions, and works closely with the teacher during summer employment.

Participating in Curriculum Development

Business leaders can be instrumental in shaping curricula. Educators should take the lead because they are more knowledgeable about curriculum development strategies; however, business leaders could provide a wealth of information and suggestions on application exercises especially regarding integrating a variety of subjects. As the world changes, the business community can provide a pulse on this change for educators and, in turn, keep the curriculum up to date. While educators are generally most knowledgeable about writing curriculum, business and industry are most knowledgeable about the competencies and skills that must be included in the curriculum if students are to be prepared to be successful, productive individuals in the global economy.

One of the major methods of business/industry participation in curriculum development is with the DACUM (developing a curriculum) process. The DACUM strategy includes business/industry representatives identifying the categories of skill and knowledge needed in specific career areas. Further information on the DACUM curriculum development strategy is included in Chapter 7.

Providing Guest Speakers and Business/Industry Tours

During classroom time, business leaders can be involved in direct teaching of the students by becoming guest speakers or hosting business/industry visits. Guest speakers can bring a sense of legitimacy to topics, helping students understand the relevance of classroom learning. Likewise, field trips can bring the classroom to life. Actually visiting a business/industry facility can help students make the link between the classroom and their future world. All these experiences can aid a student in developing a career choice.

Providing Equipment and Supplies

With the rapid changes in technology, schools often have difficulty affording state-of-the-art equipment. It can be argued that the only way the curriculum will stay current is for teachers to have the newest equipment. Businesses can be both a source of advice on which equipment is most often used and a source of support for obtaining desired equipment. Ideally, businesses will provide state-of-the-art equipment rather than hand-me-downs when they purchase new equipment. This is especially important where school-based learning dominates and the students do not get experience using modern technology in a job-based setting.

Participating in Business/School Partnerships

Many of the roles just described for business can occur within business/school partnerships. Adopt-a-school and project-driven activities are two common business/school partnership models. The adopt-a-school model is based on a single company providing resources and volunteers to a single school (Rigden, 1991). Under this model the typical pattern is for employees to meet with school officials to identify the school's needs toward which the company may be willing to contribute. Typically, whatever the school asks for, the company will provide. Businesses that are involved in adopt-a-school programs are usually financially strong and generous. The project-driven model is designed to address specific academic or social problems (Rigden, 1991). Unfortunately, these programs are often short term, and seldom implemented with the idea of producing successful results.

Job-Based Roles of Business and Industry

Providing Job-Based Learning Experiences

Providing job-based work experiences is perhaps both the largest and most difficult role for employers. We are not talking about after-school jobs in which many students currently participate. We are talking about meaningful skill-based experiences that will help students develop their job-based skills while also developing their academic skills. The School-to-Work Opportunities Act of 1994 specifically mentions work-based learning opportunities that include skills to be mastered at progressively higher levels and experiences that are relevant to a student's career major.

Summer internships at the Boeing Company are an excellent example. In the first year students receive 160 hours of broad educational training that involves an introduction to career opportunities in career management. Students use state-of-the art equipment while being exposed to production and the management skills required to run a production facility. The program also encourages teamwork among students.

Another example is Southern California Edison Company, which started a job-based program in the 1990–91 school year with only five students (Ingles, 1994). In the 1993–94 school year 44 students participated. In this program, management and unions work together to make it a success. The goal of the job-based program is for students to learn skills such as communications, problem solving, and teamwork. After every rotation, mentors, counselors, and students meet to discuss the learning that occurred and the purpose to be pursued next.

Providing Mentors and Masters

The School-to-Work Opportunities Act of 1994 specifically mentions that the work-based learning component will include workplace mentoring. In youth apprenticeship, masters will be provided for apprentices. There is doubt, however, about whether businesspeople have the time and skill to become mentors and masters on any significantly large scale. With the pressure to integrate academic and occupational content, mentors need training. Who will pay for workers' mentorship training so they can do a truly excellent job of teaching the student? Without training mentors or masters, students are likely to simply tag along with workers just learning the specifics of a job.

It is unrealistic to expect that all mentors will receive training. Therefore, the selection process for both choosing and matching a mentor and student is crucial. There are individuals in business and industry who would have a natural ability to be good mentors with minimal training. An individual who takes interest in his or her student can produce wonderful results. Schools can provide a guidebook or package of information to mentors as a useful guide. The rapport of mentor and student is extremely important. In the placement process, potential mentors and students should spend time together getting acquainted to determine if they would both be comfortable with the relationship. Smaller companies could be a rich source of mentors, and they often have a more relaxed, personal atmosphere. These companies have owners that may be interested in sharing their success and helping guide youth. Of course, this is a generalization, and appropriate selection and matching remains crucial for a successful mentorship program.

Skill Certification

Although not necessarily a role, business and industry are encouraged to support skill certification. The term *skill certificate* is defined in the School-to-Work Opportunities Act of 1994 as "a portable, industry-recognized credential issued by a School-to-Work Opportunities program under an approved State plan, that certifies that a student has mastered skills at levels that are at least as challenging as skill standards endorsed by the National Skill Standard Board." (103rd Congress, sec. 4, p.11). As these standards are developed and followed by industry, schools will need to align with these standards to provide for a smooth transition from school to work. Businesses that provide students with job-based activities will need to provide experiences that are consistent with the new national skill standards.

Role of Business and Industry in Other Countries

Because Germany and Japan are often seen as two of our major competitors in the global economy, we discuss foreign business and industry's involvement in education next. Note that we are not recommending adopting these methods. Both countries have had their problems recently. A few years ago Japan's management abilities were perceived to be superior to their U.S. counterpart. In recent years, however, Japan's image has been declining. Germany has also had problems, especially with escalating unemployment rates.

It has been estimated that U.S. workers cost $16.70 an hour, Japanese labor costs $19.30, and Germany $25.50 ("The U.S. Economy May Dominate for Years," 1994). In Germany high wages, which have led to higher unemployment, have been attributed partly to high taxes to support programs such as training. Adult retraining programs are supported by unemployment taxes that increase labor costs and drive away business. Companies in Germany complain that they retrain because labor settlements make it too expensive to lay off workers (Shlaes, 1994). Regardless, industrial jobs in Germany decreased 8% in 1993 (Shlaes, 1994).

For the last several years, the educational and business methods in both Japan and Germany have been touted as being vastly superior to those in the

United States; however, in the last year or two, job growth in the United States has increased steadily and become strong while unemployment has been high in Germany, even when figures for East Germany are excluded. At the same time, the economy in Japan is currently in flux with no easy solutions in sight. When making judgments, we must be careful to differentiate between short-term economic swings and a weak infrastructure that may result in long-term problems. Even though many of the jobs created in the United States have been low paying, Barry Bosworth, an economist at the Brookings Institution, summarizes it quite well: "The choice in large measure is between being poor in America or unemployed in Europe" (Wessel and Benjamin, p. A1).

Industry's Role in Education in Germany

Education in Germany is structured nationally with the Standard Conference of Education Ministers taking on the role of coordination. Education is managed largely by the states. Germany is committed to keeping its youth in vocational programs, a commitment that has resulted in Europe's lowest youth unemployment (Shlaes, 1994). A federal agency consults with employers and trade unions to obtain information, such as training regulations, which influence company training programs.

Over 100 total chambers in craft, agriculture, and industry are legally recognized as the experts in vocational training. Chamber vocational training committees consist of employer and union representatives along with teachers. The chambers' responsibilities cover such duties as accrediting potential training companies, registering the employer-trainee contracts, administering exams, and awarding vocational qualifications.

The dual system of apprenticeship is the dominant school-to-work method. *Dual* refers to education in both the schools and in business and industry. Students begin their apprenticeship at the age of 16. Approximately 85% of German young people in general schooling go into vocational training, with the majority entering one of the 380 different apprenticeship programs that cover trades, agriculture, industry, mining, construction, and commerce (Cheek & Campbell, 1994). Of these programs, the 25 trades most popular to men and women account for 60% and 80% of the trainees, respectively (*Vocational Education and Training in Europe*, 1992). The majority of the training locations in Germany are in small- and medium-sized companies. Most of the apprentices do not obtain employment with the contracted employer. A young person who completes an apprenticeship through the dual system is awarded a certificate.

Germany can teach the United States that industry and education can work together to help reduce youth unemployment. However, we must avoid becoming too bureaucratic. Training for the sake of training is not beneficial. It is important that training dollars be spent wisely. Training that is excessive or inefficient has just as much ability to hurt the economy as help because money is actually being wasted. Wilfried Prewo, head of the Hanover, Germany, Chamber of Commerce stated,

It's obvious to us all that retraining can protect against unemployment and that retraining is crucial in modern economies, but not when companies are forced to do it, or when it is done by a government. [And] our government neglects measures like cutting taxes or regulation. We spend a lot of money moving dead bodies around in a graveyard rather than giving breathing space to new businesses so they can grow. (Shlaes, p. A22)

Industry's Role in Education in Japan

The Japanese clearly value education as evidenced by the high respect and attractive salaries paid to teachers. Students attend school 240 days per year, approximately 33% more than U.S. students. Theory is considered very important in the vocational courses. As a result, graduates do not have the specific skills for a specialized occupation. Technical colleges do provide specialized training; however, in the first two years of the curricula, general studies constitute half of the course work.

The school path of students in Japan hinges on two main exams. First, at the end of the ninth grade, examinations determine which educational paths students may pursue. Second, after completing upper secondary education, students wanting to pursue higher education must pass an examination for the two- and four-year universities. Vocational students are those who cannot or choose not to pursue a university degree.

Work-based skills are, for the most part, deferred until the end of secondary education. Employers prefer to train recent graduates in job specifics. They want schools to help students develop appropriate attitudes and behaviors in addition to basic knowledge. Work-based education emphasizes general education. Employers view specific job training as their role.

Japanese schools and businesses work closely in placing non-college-bound youth in their first jobs. Schools (contract schools) and some employers (contract employers) have ongoing relationships. Many high school graduates are placed through this system. Job applications are controlled by schools. Employers assign a specified number of jobs to a high school. School staff select students that are appropriate for the various positions. Youth are ranked for each job opening. Grades are the primary mechanism for determining who is qualified for a position. A student who is selected can apply for the position. The contract employer may choose not to interview students who are not selected by the staff. This system has the benefit of motivating all three parties. Schools are motivated to develop and recommend students who will satisfy the needs of employers and keep them happy with the labor supply from the schools. Employers are interested in keeping a satisfactory relationship with schools so they have a good supply of high-quality workers. Students are motivated because they see the direct link between grades and becoming employed.

Like Germany, the Japanese system shows us that business/industry and education can work together. The Japanese also reinforce a few of the methods that much of the school-to-work literature discusses. First, it is crucial to make sure students perceive a connectedness between school and work; good grades will increase the chances of a good job. What a student learns will transfer into the work world, and business and industry participation can help strengthen this connectedness. Second, although job skills are critical, we should not overlook the importance of the broader academic skills that are transferable among many jobs. Business participation in providing job-based experiences must continue to develop the whole person.

Change in Attitude–What Will It Take?

There should be great concern that incentives for business are not presently available to obtain large-scale involvement by business and industry. The U.S. free enterprise system is based on making decisions that are profitable for a company. But for the majority, participating in the education of our youth would not be driven by profitability but by social consciousness. The massive change we are recommending is unlikely to occur through simple social consciousness.

As particular work-based strategies become more common and merge into other strategies or are abandoned, the type and degree of industry involvement will become more defined. Of course, which strategies become popular will be a result of the willingness of business/industry to participate. The school-based strategies are likely to be less demanding to industry than the job-based strategies. If job-based strategies become the most popular, this would imply that business and industry are playing a major role in the actual instruction of our youth. It is unlikely that job-based strategies will dominate in the near future because too many people, both educators and business leaders, would need to change their paradigms of education.

Clearly, if business is going to participate on a large scale, the educational system must be aligned to meet the needs of the business world. To oversimplify, businesses will need to realize that the benefits of their participation will exceed the costs. Businesses have options with their resources—money, people, equipment, and so on. The owners, or shareholders, in a company, generally want management to obtain a reasonable return on their investment.

Educators need to ponder the educational process from an industry—management and shareholder—perspective: Why should industry become involved? The only real answer for any businessperson is for the benefit of the company. Investors do not invest in a business to improve our educational system. If shareholders want to help education, that desire would be better served by direct support to schools. That is, individuals who want to help education financially should provide support to educational facilities rather than to companies. Shareholders invest in businesses for the financial benefit to themselves.

Shareholders expect management to maximize profitability of the firm within the "rules of the game," and, it can be argued, in a socially responsible way. The definition or interpretation of socially responsible behavior is open to debate. Regardless, management will be analyzing what is best for the company to determine whether it is wise to be active in education.

Businesses, especially where there is accountability to stockholders who are not part of management, are often criticized for making short-term decisions that are damaging to long-term profitability. However, management realizes that if short-term profits are not satisfactory, they will not be around to manage the long term. Until this mentality changes, there may be an additional hurdle before extensive business participation in education can be realized.

We have to ask: Why do companies become involved in any activity, especially community service related, outside the mainstream of their business? No one really knows the true motivation of companies; however, we can speculate that many community service activities are performed for the benefit of the company. This should come as no surprise. Shareholders and owners hire managers to manage their money for the benefit of shareholders, not society. Shareholders donate their money to charities to help society. Why do companies sponsor bike races, symphonies, tennis tournaments, and so on? We know that most companies support such activities to maintain a positive image in the community. Some companies may even donate to such activities to make their community a more appealing place to live, which may help attract top talent when recruiting for management positions. The point is, most of these activities are probably self-serving, at least partially. There is nothing wrong with these decisions or the motivations behind them; it just emphasizes the need to assure an incentive for business and industry to participate in the educational process.

Although many businesses are beginning to become involved in education, the majority of businesses remain uninvolved. This is no surprise given the infancy of the school-to-work movement. One problem that may restrain businesses from participating is that the student will not necessarily stay at the company that trains them. American society is upwardly mobile. This mobility is a two-way street. Companies are operating in a "lean and mean" fashion. Workers who are no longer productive are disposable. The following quote from a *Fortune* magazine article discussing what companies and employees owe one another summarizes the new employee-employer relationship quite well:

> There will never be job security. You will be employed by us as long as you add value to the organization, and you are continuously responsible for finding ways to add value. In return, you have the right to demand interesting and important work, the freedom and resources to perform it well, pay that reflects your contribution, and the experience and training needed to be employable here or elsewhere. (O'Reilly, p. 44).

Workers who are not treated fairly by a company look to greener pastures. People simply do not tend to stay with companies 30 years anymore. The solution is not that students must work 30 years for the company that trains them but rather that the students stay long enough so the time and money invested in them is rewarded by a reasonable length of employment. This dilemma is especially pertinent in situations where employers are providing job-based experiences for students and the employer wishes to retain the students they train.

Focusing on lack of employee loyalty, it is important that the training company treat the student fairly if the company is going to retain the student. The word *fairly* is open to much interpretation. Fairly is highly correlated with pay, especially for young people who tend to be learning the lesson that higher pay does not always offset working conditions and job satisfaction. Much of this discussion blends into human resource management. Involvement in educating students is part of recruiting, training, and hiring workers and is only one facet of a broader picture. Companies need a cohesive human resource strategy that integrates training, recruiting, selection, promotion, compensation, and so on. Without it, desirable students will tend to leave for greener pastures and training dollars will be used inefficiently.

Another area increasing the mobility of students is that the school-to-work programs need to be designed to allow students the option of pursuing further education. But this additional option results in a lower probability that the training company will obtain an adequate return on its time and money spent in training the student. Although it is true that businesses are seeing the importance of training and education even if the employee eventually leaves the company, the employee must return adequate productivity before leaving to make the training worthwhile for the company.

Osterman (1994) reported from a National Survey of Organizations that recruitment of qualified people was a major problem for only 14% of the organizations. Forty percent of the respondents reported that recruitment of qualified people was a minor problem. Forty-five percent stated that recruitment of qualified people was not a problem. Osterman also reported from a Harris survey of members of the Conference Board, made up of the largest corporations in America, that only 25% and 15% had trouble recruiting qualified high school graduates and skilled labor, respectively. Some people are likely to interpret these data as troublesome; others are likely to view these figures as satisfactory. It is clear that for many businesses finding qualified workers is very difficult. However, it appears many businesses are not having recruitment difficulties. The problem as far as educational reform is concerned is that there is not likely to be an overwhelming consensus from business and industry representatives that companies should be involved in the educational process. It is more likely to be the companies which are facing problems in recruitment of qualified workers that will want to participate in improving the educational system. It is too early to tell if these dissatisfied companies are large and motivated enough to impact much widespread change in education.

To help align schools and businesses we need to ask how businesses can benefit from participating in educating our youth. The answers will vary widely depending on the skills shortages in a particular business or industry. Imagine the typical business owner. He or she is having trouble recruiting recent graduates with the necessary skills. There are several options to consider: First, hire experienced workers in the field; second, hire and train workers that appear to have the potential to acquire many of the necessary skills; or third, participate in improving our educational process. You might decide to hire a more experienced worker, but then again, maybe there will be a shortage of such workers in the work force. Hiring and training workers may not be appealing, especially if you own a small business, because you may not have the resources for training. Of course, this may also be a problem when helping educate our youth. On the positive side, training that is job specific is typically the most cost effective.

The businessperson is likely to be interested in improving the educational system if faced with hiring people who do not appear to have the potential to acquire many of the necessary skills to be successful. It appears that the majority of companies are not in this position. However, the future may be very different. As technology evolves and jobs become broader in scope, employers may find it more difficult to hire qualified or potentially qualified employees. If this occurs, business/industry may increase their interest in the educational process.

So, let's answer the question posed in this section: Change in attitude—what will it take? The simple answer is that business and industry will have to perceive that they will benefit significantly by participating. That is, the time and money spent will amply reward the company. Although this means increasing profitability, the analysis is not that easy. Goodwill and improving the community may be good long-term strategies that improve a company's image and, in turn, increase profitability. Slightly more tangible is an educated work force that companies can use. Also, businesses can have input into what is being taught in our schools. Simply stated, investing in education is investing in the infrastructure of our country. Traditionally our infrastructure has been built by government programs through taxes. If business and industry believe they are needed to develop a globally competitive work force, they will participate. The evidence suggests, however, that some businesses are interested and others are not.

Thus, arrangements such as the Detroit Compact discussed in Chapter 4 seem to be the win-win solution. The Detroit Compact is administered by the Greater Detroit Chamber of Commerce and involves businesses, community groups, state and city governments, and organized labor. In Boston and Louisville, the business community is organized around work and school issues (Osterman, 1994). Companies can be approached as a group.

Another similar method is to seek industry help through organizations such as the National Tooling and Machining Association (Osterman, 1994). Most industries have organizations developed around the industry. The companies in industries that have trouble recruiting qualified workers are likely to be motivated to work together to strengthen the labor force.

The rationale for forming groups rather than individual companies stems from the fact that the interests of the business community, in aggregate, are likely to be disjointed. The sectors of the economy that are interested in participating can work together with other interested parties. The entities that become involved can treat their activities as a way to develop a stronger labor pool and a method of employee recruitment. This is not to say there are not altruistic reasons for participating. However, more than just altruism is needed to motivate a large number of companies.

Using business organizations may be the best option because, otherwise, involvement may be too staggered. This structure can be the foundation that forms a win-win situation: Both schools and companies will benefit. Through the use of organizations, interested companies can pool resources to spread the demands of time and money on their resources. This coordinated effort can increase the likelihood of participation by some businesses. Therefore, a synergistic effect takes place; by combining cooperative businesses a more coordinated effort can occur with a greater number of companies participating. Joint cooperation among companies appears to be a major part of the solution for obtaining widespread involvement of business and industry.

Additional Barriers

Supervisory costs such as student attendance and behavioral management of students have been a problem to companies participating in youth apprenticeship and school-to-work pilot programs (Bailey, 1994, from Pauley, Kopp, & Haimson, 1994). It has even been argued that supervisory costs were greater barriers to employer participation than the actual cost of student wages (Bailey, 1994, from Hershey & Silverberg, 1993). This suggests that for job-based experiences to be successful, students need to be reliable, well-behaved workers and trainees. Unfortunately, this may be an unrealistic expectation. There are likely to be students who abuse privileges. What employers are willing to tolerate will vary. So schools have the difficult task of making sure students behave on the job site. One hope is that the job-based experiences will gain a reputation among students as being excellent, thereby giving students an incentive to meet job site requirements. Before a good reputation is developed, the transition stage will probably be difficult.

Historically, companies are not as interested in hiring a new young graduate versus the worker with experience. There is a chicken versus the egg debate. Businesspeople will argue that the recent graduate is more likely to be a job hopper, unreliable, and possessing limited skills. Although this may be true, students may be unskilled and unmotivated to learn because they do not see that their education will lead to employment. Which came first, the unskilled and unreliable student or the lack of opportunity? This question is open to debate and probably not of much significance because all it answers is who is to blame. It is much wiser to figure out how we, as a society, will fix the problem. While there will be no overnight solutions, work-based learning has the opportunity to minimize this problem. As industry plays a larger role in preparing students, their suspicions can be minimized. Training students is an excellent method for evaluating potential workers before submitting an offer of employment. The opportunity to evaluate students over a long period of time is likely to result in a better match in the hiring process. Work-based experiences for students will result in a better prepared individual for the workplace. Therefore, companies should become more satisfied with younger workers.

Large companies such as Boeing, Toyota, and General Motors have more resources for educating and training. Unfortunately, large businesses are downsizing and the small- and medium-sized businesses are growing. Most people are employed by smaller companies. In many geographic areas, there are no large businesses. Smaller businesses may not even have a human resources department. These businesses tend to be a little "leaner and meaner." Oftentimes the human resources are not available to help in the educational process. Many of these companies cannot even find the time or resources to train their own people.

There is much talk about treating employees as assets rather than costs. One aspect of this is investing in employees through training. However, most training is invested in the more highly educated white-collar employees. As workers continue to be expected to be more flexible and have broader skills, there will be pressure to train workers already employed. It is natural to expect businesses to increase training of their own employees before they take on training of students.

How to Motivate the Business World

Many alternatives are being discussed about how to get the business world involved. When government wants to manipulate the way business makes decisions, tax incentives or tax credits are often proposed. When there was a shortage of real estate, there were generous tax incentives to motivate the business community to build homes and apartments and develop commercial property. A possibility for training our youth is to provide a tax credit to business/industry for participating in the training process.

If the government is motivated to force business to participate, simple taxes are levied. Although not a tax in the strictest sense, Bill Clinton ran for office prepared to force businesses to spend a percentage of their payroll on training. Mandating business to spend money on training is probably not wise because business owners are most likely to know the best use for their money. There is an old saying, "No one else would spend my money the way I will." That is, businesses know their needs, wants, and desires more than anyone else, and therefore should decide the best way to spend their money. In addition, payroll-type taxes increase payroll expenses, which can provide a disincentive for companies to expand their labor force. These inefficient policies are some of the problems that Germany is facing.

Government intervention of this nature has its own philosophical and political problems. In essence, these programs are tinkering with the free enterprise system, which can always be dangerous. Special interest groups will be involved. Power and compromise can lead to a less than satisfactory tax incentive package.

Given all the problems we have discussed, the involvement of business and industry through industry associations, organizations, and other broader entities seems to be a part of the win-win solution. Organizations are increasingly becoming supportive of school-to-work strategies to develop and implement industry skill standards (Bailey, 1994, from McNeil, 1993). Programs that strengthen the labor pool in industries that have a shortage of skilled workers provide an atmosphere where all parties involved will benefit.

Summary

Clearly, there are many hurdles to obtaining full involvement of business and industry for the greatest success of work-based learning. Educators cannot turn away from these hurdles—they must view business/industry participation from the businessperson's point of view. Working from this perspective will help develop a win-win educational process for all.

Despite all these hurdles, there are many companies that are getting involved in education. Since the National Alliance of Business formed a school-to-work center in 1993, it has received more than 700 calls from business and industry people who are interested in participating in education ("Quid Pro Quo," 1994). Although there has not been extensive research on why business and industry participate, much of what has been discussed in this chapter hints at the reasons. In essence, participation in the educational system is a method of recruiting, training, and hiring workers. Companies that have a foreseeable need for workers in which the supply is scarce are more likely to participate. Other companies may participate simply to be involved and help society.

In the late 1980s rapid growth at Boeing resulted in the hiring of many inexperienced workers as a result of a shortage of skilled labor (Kreitner, 1992). In the short run, Boeing had to transfer experienced workers from their military aircraft division. Part of Boeing's long-term strategy was to invest more heavily in training. Boeing clearly had a vested interest in increasing their training. Likewise, because Boeing had trouble recruiting skilled labor, they have a vested interest in helping educate the youth of this country. It is a good recruiting technique and an excellent method for evaluating potential workers. Again, this is not to say there are not also altruistic reasons for Boeing's participation. The idea of killing two birds with one stone makes a lot of sense for any company who wants to help society. The point is it helps to have both altruistic and economic reasons to motivate any business to participate.

In theory it is quite simple to obtain business and industry involvement on a large scale. In practice it will probably prove to be difficult. If there is one simple truth to this chapter, it is this:

To play a major role in the educational system, business and industry must perceive that they are benefiting from the time and money expended.

References

Bailey, T. (1994). *Barriers to Employer Participation in School-to-Work Transition Programs*. Paper prepared for a seminar, "Employer Participation in School-to-Work Transition Programs," the Brookings Institution, Washington, DC.

Cheek, G. D., & Campbell, C. P. (1994). "School-to-Work Lessons from Abroad." *Tech Directions 53*(7), pp. 11–21.

Council of Chief State School Officers. (1992). *Connecting School and Employment: Policy Statement 1991*. Washington, DC: Author.

Ingles, P. (1994). "Electric Avenue: A Utility Company's Work Experience Program Broadens Opportunities for Students." *American Vocational Journal 69*(5), pp. 28–30.

Kreitner, R. (1992). *Management* (5th ed.). Boston: Houghton Mifflin.

103rd Congress. School-to-Work Opportunities Act of 1994, sec. 4, H.R. 2884.

O'Reilly, B. (1994). "The New Deal: What Companies and Employees Owe One Another." *Fortune 129*(12), pp. 44–47, 50, 52.

Osterman, P. (1994). *Strategies for Involving Employers in School to Work Programs.* Prepared for a conference at the Brookings Institution, Washington, DC.

"Quid Pro Quo." (1994). *Vocational Education Journal 69*(5), pp. 22–23, 39.

Rigden, D. W. (1991). *Business/School Partnerships: A Path to Effective School Restructuring.* New York: Council for Aid to Education.

Shlaes, A. (April 26, 1994). " 'Re-employment' That Kills Jobs." *Wall Street Journal*, p. A22.

"The U.S. Economy May Dominate for Years." (January 10, 1994). *Wall Street Journal*, p. A1.

Vocational Education and Training in Europe. A Four-Country Study in Four Employment Sectors. (1992). London: Further Education Unit (ED 353 473).

Wessel, D., & Benjamin, D. (1994, March 14). "Looking for Work: In Employment Policy, America and Europe Make a Sharp Contrast." *Wall Street Journal*, pp. A1–A5.

Chapter 9

Professional Development for Work-Based Learning

"If we succeed in reforming education . . . . it will be because teachers and professors alike have been empowered to replace old attitudes and concepts with new ones. The development of these attitudes and concepts must be our first concern."
(Duffy, 1994)

Lisa Smith (fictitious name) has been a math teacher for two decades. Over 20 years ago she attended a university to pursue a teaching degree. During her program of study, she learned how to teach math. When she did her student teaching, experienced teachers helped her develop teaching skills to become an excellent teacher. Upon graduation, she obtained a position teaching math in a suburban high school. She used her math textbooks and supporting materials to prepare for classes. Of course, the textbooks contained a lot of math problems. The few word problems presented were related to two trains coming from opposite directions at various speeds and other such fairly standard situations. She neither learned how her subject area is applied in the world of work nor thought about integrating math with other subjects. The emphasis was clearly on learning math, not on how to use math.

Whenever Lisa needed help with teaching, she approached the veteran teachers who had similar teacher preparation backgrounds. Of course, there are requirements to maintain her certification. So she takes a few courses every couple of years and obtains information similar to what she was exposed to as an undergraduate. When she is lucky enough to go to conferences, she is sur-rounded by people who have backgrounds similar to hers.

Today, Lisa and her colleague, Dave Brown (fictitious name), a science teacher, attended an in-service professional development program where the speaker talked about work-based learning. She has read about work-based learning and it makes some sense to her. At the end of the speaker's presentation, Lisa raised her hand and asked, "This all sounds good, but I have never worked a day in my life outside of teaching (with the exception of high school and college jobs); I don't have the knowledge to teach in an applied, work-based manner. What do you suggest?"

After the in-service presentation, Dave tells Lisa, "The information was pretty interesting, but after all these years of teaching, I'm not going to change now. Science is a difficult subject . . . some people get it [the college bound] and others don't."

Lisa has been somewhat frustrated by her students' lack of motivation and is searching for new ideas. She is willing to try anything. Dave is set in his ways. He is content enough with his teaching results that he sees no reason to change. After all, he is getting through to his favorite students.

Professional Development: The Master Key

Throughout the book, we have been discussing the keys to work-based learning; however, the master key, the key of all keys, to making work-based learning succeed is professional development because it has the potential to open all the doors (e.g., counseling, curriculum development, philosophical changes) for creating the necessary linkage between school and work. Without professional development, the chance of any significant change is remote.

To alter the analogy a bit, professional development could be considered a bank safety deposit key. With a safety deposit box, two keys are needed to open the box—the customer's and the bank's. Without both, the box will never open. Without professional development, teachers, counselors, administrators, curricula, and all the other boxes will never open.

In an October 1992 seminar in New Orleans, Jim Hoerner was making a presentation to 80 business and industry people and asked the question, "If you decided to change your product or service, what would be the first thing you would do?" The response from an audience member was "extensive staff development and training for those producing the product or service." If a business is going to change its product or service, it goes without saying that extensive retraining of those producing the product or service will take place. The changes we propose are a major change in the product or service we are delivering. It is analogous to changing a production facility from dairy to orange juice production. Although your customers may be the same, the product is different and production methods are different.

How can we expect educators to produce a different product and produce the new product in a new way? The only answer that makes sense is professional development that starts with explaining the benefits of work-based learning. We are not talking about making a unilateral decision about the direction of our educational system. We realize this will not work. Educators must believe in their own hearts that work-based education is superior to content-based education. Frankly, this conversion is not an easy task. As we have said, it requires a paradigm shift, a rethinking of what educators have thought and been taught. We must prepare educators to teach in a different way.

How much longer can we tolerate preparing teachers without an emphasis on practical application? It is reasonable to assume that educators are in the business of preparing students to be successful in environments where 90% or more of educators have never been. Would our society tolerate professors of medicine who had never practiced as physicians teaching in the medical schools? How about pilots? We would hate to think people who have never flown a plane are teaching pilots how to fly. Where is the logic in having teachers prepare people for careers in which they have had little or no experience?

Educators just need to be astute, erudite individuals in their discipline if education is not meant to be practical. However, if education is to have application to the real world where most students will need to make a living, educators must obtain experience in noneducation settings. In our opinion, teachers should have three areas of competency: (1) knowledge of content area, (2) knowledge of content utilization; and (3) competence in the art and skill of facilitating learning. Although areas 1 and 3 are often cited, 2 is usually missing. For the second competency to enter the educational system mainstream, educators must evolve and accept that understanding content utilization is important. Educators who still believe in content-based learning will have to go through a seven-step process before work-based learning succeeds.

From Awareness to Action: A Seven-Step Model

Figure 9.1 illustrates a seven-step model that can be useful when developing a professional development plan: awareness, knowledge, interest, acceptance, preference, conviction, and action. The primary application of this model is to analyze at which stage people or a whole school system are with regard to work-based learning. This can drive the type of professional development activities provided.

The first step to bringing about any change is *awareness*. If educators are not aware of work-based learning concepts, they obviously cannot adopt them. Because of the educational backgrounds of most teachers (discussed later in the

Figure 9.1

Awareness to Action: A Seven-Step Model

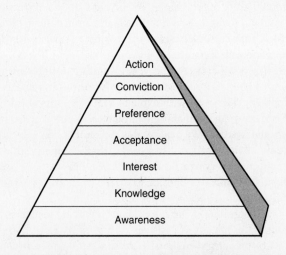

chapter), awareness may not be high; however, with the support of President Clinton and his administration and a reasonably large body of literature discussing work-based learning, most educators are becoming aware. The important point at this stage is that educators are well enough informed to understand that work-based learning is an option. Professional development can increase awareness by clarifying the work-based learning concept.

It is commonly held that 75% of the jobs by the year 2000 will not require a four-year degree. This is not to say these job holders will not need high-level skills. Most people will need practical education beyond high school, but not a baccalaureate degree. How many high school educators recognize that approximately 75% of their students must become successful, productive individuals in careers that do not require a baccalaureate degree? This is the type of initial information that must be brought home to educators.

The second step, *knowledge*, is important to move educators toward making a decision about whether work-based learning has appeal. Without knowledge, it is difficult to have a positive opinion. Professional development can inform educators about the benefits of work-based learning.

If the knowledge provided in step 2 makes sense, educators will develop *interest*, which will lead to searching out more information and possibly experimentation. Teachers may want to meet to discuss the purpose of our educational system and other related matters. Professional development can be a mechanism that supports such activities.

Interest can lead to *acceptance*. In the acceptance stage, momentum can build with additional experimentation in work-based teaching techniques. Teachers can share each other's successes, triumphs, and even frustrations. The enthusiasm of educators can lead to acceptance by other educators. Professional development that provides teachers with the time to share their ideas and concerns is essential.

Acceptance can lead to *preference*. That is, educators will believe in their hearts that drawing connections between school and work is a more relevant, timely philosophy than content-based learning. This may occur through simple knowledge attainment or through actually applying new techniques that are successful. Every educator will be different. The key is to convince the majority of educators of the superiority of work-based learning. Professional development plays a big role through providing information and letting educators work together to solve problems.

A word of caution: Even if the majority of educators prefer work-based learning, a change in behavior is not guaranteed. That is, educators must have a burning desire or *conviction* that they are willing to change their *actions* to match their beliefs. It is unclear whether Brown, the science teacher, believes in work-based learning. However, his lack of desire to change undermines his motivation to alter his teaching style. With such a mind-set the benefits of work-based learning must be reiterated and attempts made to prompt these educators to act on their newfound convictions.

This model can be applied to school systems and individuals. Clearly, individuals will go through these stages at different speeds. Some people can go up to the action stage in one day and start application the following day. Other people will be harder to convince, and years may pass before interest occurs.

From the standpoint of implementing professional development activities, it is important to determine at which stage the teachers, as a whole, are regarding work-based learning. This will dictate what type of professional development is needed. If a high percentage of teachers are not familiar with work-based learning, professional development should focus first on awareness or knowledge. If a high percentage of teachers are close to the action step, it is imperative to support teachers with how-to activities that will help them become successful.

When allocating professional development funds, there is a fine balance between selling the concept of building connections between school and work and providing educators with the ability to teach in this manner. Even early on, some professional development funds should be spent on training teachers how to implement work-based learning. This is important to reduce frustration for those who are experimenting in the beginning stages. If the initial experiments are successful, other educators will be encouraged to experiment. However, if the how-to is emphasized before teachers are convinced, success is not likely. Educators are likely to feel they are being forced to teach according to a concept they do not believe in.

The attitudes of Lisa Smith and Dave Brown are prevalent in our educational system. Professional development must address both. Specifically, professional development can (1) help educators shift their paradigm about education; and (2) help teachers obtain the skills to be able to teach the connections. Both of these areas focus on in-service professional development, which focuses on education and training for teachers presently in the teaching field. However before discussing in-service, a discussion on preservice is prudent, since this is where the preparation of teachers begins. Preservice is the education and training of people to prepare them to become teachers.

Preservice in Colleges of Education–Is There Hope?

Preservice traditionally consists of a teacher education program at a college or university. While changing the way teacher education programs are structured is very important, it is a very slow method of change. The typical career lasts approximately 40 years (from age 25 to 65). Thus every 10 years one fourth of the personnel turns over. Although this may not be exact because of demographic trends, it paints the picture that the majority of people who will be educators in the beginning of the next century are already teachers today. A broader statistic often cited is that more than 85% of those who will be working in the year 2001 are in the work force today (Werther & Davis, 1993). There is no reason to believe the statistics would vary significantly for educators.

We have emphasized that all educators must make a mind-set change about the purpose of our schools. To this point, we have not looked closely at teacher education programs or the professors who provide these programs. Like our example of Lisa Smith at the beginning of the chapter, our educators are being taught and molded by college of education professors, or teacher educators, who do not believe the purpose of our schools is to prepare people for work or life. If education professors do not alter their paradigms, there is little hope their protégés going out into the schools will be changing.

It would be invaluable for students pursuing an education degree to spend time in a business environment. Preservice teacher education could involve programs built around spending time out in the world of work. But the only way teacher education programs will evolve to anything remotely similar to this is if education professors believe in positive connections between school and work.

So how do we convince teacher educators that work-based learning is now more appropriate than content-based learning? The answer is proof. Most professors expect research to back up theories before they are willing to accept them as fact. Work-based learning makes intuitive sense, but because of its infancy, the facts are not conclusive that work-based learning will solve the problems in education. The initial phase of a paradigm shift requires acting on faith before proof is available. So we have catch-22. Professors are not willing to buy into work-based learning until there is proof, and work-based learning cannot succeed until education professors are persuaded to revamp teacher education programs. This sobering news suggests that change will have to occur in baby steps. Some positive results will need to trickle in as reformers of the educational system slowly gather allies. This slow process should come as no surprise because our educational system has been content-based for such a long time.

There are ways the process can accelerate. The specific method we have in mind can be called a pull strategy, which entails parents, teachers, and businesspeople complaining that the educational system is not doing the job. We have already acknowledged that adults do not feel the educational system is adequately preparing people for work and life. If all educators, including education professors, feel there is enough wrong with the current system, they may re-evaluate the purpose of our educational system. Because of the training and background of most professors, we do not foresee a pull strategy effecting change. Most professors will not change their minds based on the opinions or desires of others. They require proof. Most professors are not willing to step out and embrace any paradigm shift in the early stages. The marketing phrase "find a need and fill it" is foreign to many professors. In education terms, professors are traditionally not trained to seek and fill the needs and wants of students and related entities (e.g., parents, students, businesses). Most professors have been trained to look at research to determine solutions to problems.

By glancing at the classified advertisements in *The Chronicle of Higher Education* it appears that universities do try to recruit education professors who have school teaching experience. Although this is good news, there are many education professors who have no public school teaching experience. We must ask: How can education professors expect to teach future teachers if they have never experienced the environment in which their students will make a living? Teacher educators may need to spend more time in the schools.

Equally disappointing are the supervisors who evaluate student teachers. Too often supervisors are graduate students who have little or no experience with school teaching. This does not appear to be the wisest way to train teachers.

Most businesses will train new recruits with successful individuals, not with other new employees who are just learning themselves. If a company were to train new sales recruits, it would be more likely that a successful or experienced salesperson would do the training. It would be highly improbable that the salesperson just out of training would then train the new recruits.

Many professors, both in education and other fields, have not experienced applications of their discipline. When colleges or universities recruit faculty, educational background is typically much more important than work experience, which is often considered nice but unnecessary. Many professors will never experience firsthand how their content is applied. If education is to be application oriented, this must change. We are talking about nothing less than a revolution within our colleges of education.

In-Service Training

How can we ask current educators to shift to a work-based mode if they have only been prepared to teach content? The majority of teachers, counselors, administrators, and other educators presently view the educational system as content-based without linkages to the world of work. A workshop participant of Jim Hoerner's commented, "I have taught science for 12 years and nobody even suggested it [talking to business and industry about how science is applied] or [it] never occurred to me to talk to business or industry to see applications of science." Until we unlock the idea that schools should be linked to the world of life and work, and educators become believers, no change will occur in this system. As the saying goes, "If you keep doing what you are doing, you will keep getting what you are getting."

One of the dilemmas is that the majority of current educators have not had substantial employment experience outside of education; therefore, they do not have the employment experience in the various employment settings where the majority of their students will need to be successful. In-service training is useful for maintaining knowledge and facilitating growth. In the context of work-based learning, it can be the critical tool to large-scale change in the schooling process. Once teachers are convinced to draw connections between school and work, professional development activities should be provided to help teachers and other educators get the taste, smell, and feel of the environments that the majority of their students will occupy upon graduation. A variety of methods can be used:

- field trips
- business and industry mentors for faculty
- vocational/academic education buddies
- business/industry experience on a rotation basis
- business/industry internships
- "Work-a-Day" in industry programs
- university independent studies

This aspect of professional development is critical. If educators begin to see that work-based learning is an effective strategy, but implementation falls short, they are likely to get discouraged. The biggest mistake would be to have a significant change in belief, but inadequate professional development. Activities must be provided to aid teachers in acquiring the skills to teach in an applied, contextual manner.

Teacher Certification

Teacher certification (i.e., state licensure and teacher credentials) traditionally involves teachers enrolling in six hours of college coursework in their discipline every five years. Some states are allowing in-service activities to count as part of teacher recertification. Returning to a college or university to obtain more knowledge about a discipline is not likely to be the best method for growth. Those teachers already strong in content, which we suspect is true in the majority of cases, are better off obtaining experience in the world of work. We must go beyond going back to the university for recertification when the value added is questionable.

We propose that teachers can *only* become recertified by participating in business or industry for a minimum of five months every five years. This is not to say that other recertification methods cannot be used in conjunction with obtaining business or industry experience; however, we are recommending that part of recertification must entail obtaining noneducation experience. The specific time, five months of experience for five years, is somewhat arbitrary. The key here is not the time as much as the quality of experience in the real world of business and industry. We use these figures as a starting point for others to discuss and debate.

Professional Development for All Teachers

Our focus may appear to be solely on high school and postsecondary levels. However let there be no mistake, we are talking about including all teachers, elementary teachers through university. Why not? After all, we live in a work-oriented society. Education should be about relating content to life and ultimately being a productive individual someday. The point is that whatever the content, at whatever level, there should be some connectedness to life and making a living.

In Chagrin Falls, Ohio, third graders at Sands Elementary School set up a snack counter for a school movie. While it may appear to be a rather simple project, the learning that occurred was tremendous. The students obtained a $200 loan from a bank and purchased inventory—candy, popcorn, and Kool-Aid. When the kids wanted to eat the inventory, the teachers discussed the consequences. If the profits were not available, the students were responsible for repaying the debt. They even forecast their profitability, which went toward a worthy cause chosen by the children. Recent profits have been invested in an acre of rain forest, the local historical society, and flowerpots for mothers on

Mother's Day (Murray, 1994). Just such a simple project can result in the students developing skills such as critical thinking, decision making, communications, and teamwork, to name a few, and all are required in life and the work force. As this example shows, there are methods for relating subject matter at any educational level to the students' futures.

"I Don't Have Time for Professional Development"

Due to time constraints, summer professional development appears to be an important part of the puzzle. This solution may not be appealing to many teachers, especially those who choose teaching in order to have their summers free. One possibility is for teachers to be on a 12-month contract with part of the summer spent in business and industry. Obviously, a change of this magnitude would be met with much resistance. Whether it is feasible is another question. This contract would require more pay, and budgets are already tight. With the aging population, the financial support for education is not likely to strengthen. Regardless, the concept of a 12-month contract is worth discussing and debating throughout the country.

Summary

Much of this chapter may seem to be pie-in-the-sky thinking. We are fully aware of the magnitude of the change we are proposing. How many educators are willing to put forth the effort it will take to really change the schooling process? Throughout the writing of this book, we have asked ourselves this question many times. Many people are going to resist. The primary way to reduce resistance is through education, which is why professional development is the master key.

Professional development is the engine that can drive educators to believe in a school system that prepares students for work and life. Without professional development, our system will not move. We commend the hard-working teachers in the United States. Teachers have been trained to teach in a content-based manner. Professional development provides the opportunity for educators to rethink the purpose of our schools and alter the system. This is an exciting time to question all of our thinking, all of our past paradigms.

We believe the majority of students and parents would support a change in our educational system. Now educators need to listen to their customers to determine if they should shift their paradigm about the purpose of schools. For educators who believe in work-based learning, professional development must be provided so their actions can match their new paradigms.

Let us make no mistake. This challenge to change people's minds is no easy task. People do not like change. Teachers and other educators must become discontented. They must feel the problems are great enough that another method is worth trying. Many times, before change occurs, things have to get worse before they get better. As long as educators have a comfort level and are content, it may be extremely difficult to build interest in other alternatives. As negative as it may sound, we hope there are sufficient numbers of unhappy educators willing to look at other alternatives. We hope educators are not blaming students because they are then unlikely to see any serious problems with our schooling process. As the saying goes, "When you point a finger at someone else, you have three other fingers that point right back at you."

Dynamic professional development is the master key that must be used to unlock the potential of work-based learning. Without extensive professional development, work-based learning and school-to-work transition will not succeed.

References

Duffy, G. (1994). "Professional Development Schools and the Disempowerment of Teachers and Professors." *Phi Delta Kappan 75*(8), pp. 596–600.

Murray, M. (1994, April, 29). "When Mom Taught Business 101, She Paid for the Lemonade Herself." *Wall Street Journal*, p. B1.

Werther, W. B., & Davis, K. (1993). *Human Resource and Personnel Management* (4th ed.). New York: McGraw-Hill.

Chapter 10

Steps and Strategies for Implementing Work-Based Learning

"To the extent that the reality of the educational environment is vastly different than the reality of the work environment, we are creating difficulty for the transition from school-to-work."
(Jim Hoerner)

Work-based learning and school-to-work transition represent concepts of learning that have the ability to impact the total schooling process. All educators must change the way things have always been done. As the new paradigm for the future schooling process is invented in the United States, many groups will need to assume new roles. This chapter is a collection of steps, strategies, and roles that will assist various groups and individuals as they implement the concepts of work-based learning and school-to-work transition for all students. The various lists are not meant to be sequential or all inclusive. It is our intent that these lists will help jog educators' minds and guide them in implementing a work-based learning system. We believe the key groups for implementing work-based learning and school-to-work transition programs are classroom teachers, career guidance and counseling personnel, administrators, and business and industry personnel. The following sections discuss each of these groups.

Classroom Teachers

Although many people play important roles in education, the most vital player on the school-to-work transition team is the classroom teacher. The classroom teachers who interface with students every day have more impact on our young people than any other single group. They can greatly influence attitudes and feelings in areas such as the following:

- relevancy and applications of knowledge
- working for a living
- lifelong learning
- individual achievement and self-esteem

- acceptance of responsibility
- cooperation and teamwork

What is imperative is that classroom teachers, as well as all educators, first recognize and accept the importance of a positive connection between school and work. Once this philosophical hurdle is crossed, there are a number of steps, strategies, and roles for classroom teachers to implement the concepts of work-based learning and school-to-work transition for all students.

Steps, Strategies, and Roles for the Classroom Teacher

1. *Become a believer and champion for work-based learning and school-to-work transition programs for all students.* This step entails a philosophical mind-set change that each teacher has to make if he or she is going to be a change agent in the schooling process. It will probably not happen until each teacher reexamines the purpose of education today and rethinks the whole schooling process. Participation in professional development activities that address school-to-work opportunities and visits to modern businesses and industries are key activities to help with this mind-set change.

2. *Join an integrated vocational and academic team.* One of the best ways to implement this step is for each teacher to select two or three other teachers from different disciplines. We suggest that the team include math, science, communications, and vocational teachers to work together. An example is a high school team in the Milwaukee system that has four teachers representing mathematics, science, language arts, and technology education.

3. *Talk with as many business and industry personnel as you can to obtain applications of content.* Today's educators must be aware of the applications of their content area in the real world. They also need to be cognizant of the kinds of work environments in which their students will need to be successful. Because most current classroom teachers, especially the academic teachers, have had little experience outside of education, this strategy could be one of the most beneficial professional development experiences. We believe every educator ought to have meaningful business and industry experiences to develop the awareness needed to form the connections now required between school and work. Examples of these experiences are Work-a-Day in industry programs, industry mentors for teachers, and summer employment. In Chapter 9 seven different strategies were outlined that should provide this sort of meaningful experience. The Milwaukee team mentioned in number 2 spent one month in industry as a team before launching their program. Initial contacts with business and industry can be made through the local Chamber of Commerce or business organizations.

4. *Assess the content of what you are teaching and why students need to know it for their future lives.* When moving from content-based learning to applied, contextual work-based learning, examine very closely what students are expected to learn and how it is relevant to their future lives. This step or strategy is probably new for most educators. Although many will challenge this idea, we suggest pondering this thought: If we as classroom teachers cannot support with sound rationale why our students should learn something, how can we expect

our students to feel they should learn it? To say, "because it is in the book" or "you will need it to go to college" or "to pass the test" are not adequate reasons. If you cannot provide a convincing rationale, we challenge you whether it should be learned, at least at this time. To start, some tough questions must be posed: Are the assessment instruments geared to measure true knowledge of a particular concept to the end that the student is qualified in that area? Is the curriculum geared to that assessment technique? Will the students and their goals benefit by the curriculum and assessment? Are the curriculum and assessment relevant to the students' career major and path?

5. *Participate with the team to identify applications of content in the "real world."* As a result of business/industry visits and working as a team, applications of content to the "real world" can be developed. It may be desirable to have a business/industry representative on your team to help determine applications periodically.

6. *Develop joint integrated lessons and units of instruction.* It is imperative that the team develop integrated lessons and units of instruction that tie the different disciplines together. Integrated lessons and units of instruction should be thematic and relate to broad scenarios and applications that link the concepts of the various content areas together. Themes such as problem solving, teamwork, and cooperation cut across math, science, and language arts quite well. The SCANS "workplace know-how skills" discussed in Chapter 7 and illustrated in Figures 7.2 and 7.3 are broad themes that lend themselves well to integrated units of instruction.

7. *Design units of instruction around themes and projects relating to applications.* The themes discussed in number 6 can be used for broad-based projects that relate to the integrated units. The projects provide opportunity to apply the concepts and themes across disciplines. For example, the Milwaukee team had the students develop promotional packages for public relations. Students worked as cooperative learning teams developing video advertisements, scripts, promotional materials, and so on. Math, science, and language arts as well as technology skills were fully integrated in the projects.

8. *Implement applied, contextual learning strategies.* With this strategy we are suggesting developing hands-on contextual activities for learning. Many themes and projects are appropriate. Activities and projects in science and vocational labs that integrate math and communication skills are excellent for applied learning strategies. The work-based strategies we discussed in Chapter 4, both the school-based strategies and job-based strategies, are excellent strategies for applied learning. We encourage you to review them for further ideas.

9. *Ask students to identify uses/applications for what they are learning.* To help students recognize the relevancy of their studies, ask them to think of and identify uses and applications. They can check with family and friends for such applications. Students who have experienced industrial field trips, shadowing, part-time employment, mentorships, co-op experiences, and apprenticeship experiences can relate uses and applications of what they are studying in given academic courses.

10. *Believe in and contribute to the development of career majors for all students.* The School-to-Work Opportunities Act of 1994 recommends that such majors be declared no later than the eleventh grade level. It is not unreasonable to assume that greater connections between school and work at all grade levels would result in the majority of students having a good idea of their career interests. Whether a student is interested in becoming a physician, scientist, carpenter, or machinist their education would be far more meaningful if they had a career major to work toward.

11. *Support and participate in articulated seamless career paths that link elementary, secondary, and postsecondary levels including community colleges and universities.* All educators must recognize their roles in the articulated seamless career paths of their students. The scope of thinking for educators must be broader than the discipline and grade levels they are teaching. Both the fourth grade elementary and ninth grade algebra teacher need to think beyond what they are teaching to the role they are playing in the career development continuum of their students as discussed in Chapter 6 (Figure 6.2).

12. *Support career cluster concepts, which include both university-driven careers and nonuniversity careers in the same cluster pathway.* Dual tracking of "career bound" or "college bound" must be eliminated and replaced with broad career clusters that can include all students. Because careers have different levels of preparation, the key point is that all students are in career cluster pathways with multiple exits.

13. *Pursue restructuring the school schedule to set up block schedules, team teaching, and so on.* As we move to work-based learning and integrated career pathways, new schooling schedules will be critical. Block schedules and team teaching will be more common. Career academies and school-based enterprises will be used to provide integrated curriculum. The Milwaukee team has four class periods of 100 students during which they teach math, science, language arts, and technology education.

14. *Identify and develop work-based learning activities—school-based and job-based, for example, co-op, part-time employment, summer employment, school-based enterprise activities, internships, clinics, simulated experiences, mock business/industry activities, and apprenticeships.* If we believe school and work should be connected, then all kinds of work-based experiences must be provided for all students. It is time that all teachers consider methods of tearing down the walls between school and work. *All* students should now experience hands-on activities based on work settings. The future physician, lawyer, or engineer should have shadowing, mentoring, internships, part-time employment, and other business or industry experience just like the future computer technician or machinist.

15. *Form partnerships with business/industry.* One of the themes of the School-to-Work Opportunities Act of 1994 is to develop connections between school and work. The best way to do this is to develop greater partnerships of all types with business and industry. Such partnerships can take place through curriculum development activity, work-based learning experiences for students,

school/industry advisory committees, and faculty professional development business/industry experiences. The local Chamber of Commerce or small business organizations can provide initial contacts for the exploration of partnerships.

16. *Link instruction with the students' Individual Career Development Plans (ICDPs).* As discussed in Chapter 5, one of the major weaknesses in the American system is the absence of career counseling. A major tool for enhancing career counseling would be for all students to have an Individual Career Development Plan (ICDP). For ICDPs to be effective, teachers need to relate their instruction whenever possible to their students' career plans. All teachers could easily ask students about their ICDPs and then relate their lessons to such career pursuits. This can take place as early as the third grade (see the 16 components for an ICDP in Chapter 5).

17. *Participate in the development of promotional materials for parents and community.* As work-based learning is developed, parents and the community will need to be apprised of the changes. Faculty will want to participate in writing brochures, producing videos, developing flyers, and sponsoring media spots to help promote the new educational paradigm.

18. *Participate in a school-to-work transition steering committee at your school.* Change takes champions and teams of individuals to make things happen. Each school should develop a school-based school-to-work steering committee to provide the direction and energy needed. The committee should consist of teachers, counselors, administrators, and business/industry representatives to steer the reform. For best results, the team should be initiated by and involve the persons on staff committed to work-based learning for school-to-work transition.

19. *Collect and share applied, contextual learning resources.* Teachers need to collect and share books, articles, videos, applied instructional materials, and other work-based learning and school-to-work transition resources. It is important to always realize work-based learning and school-to-work transition is a united, team-based reform movement.

20. *Be a catalyst for change.* Simply stated, be a pioneer for change. Good educational reform and new paradigms take pioneers for change. We hope you (the reader) are one.

Career Guidance and Counseling Personnel

Guidance and counseling personnel play a significant role in creating an atmosphere that supports preparing everyone for life and the real world. Guidance and counseling are not activities that only occur in the counselor's office. What must be achieved is a climate and atmosphere where all educators participate in helping students choose and develop careers. This emphasis on career development should be part of the total school environment that offers success-oriented career pathways through which students become self-supporting, productive, contributing members of society. When students experience this climate of success, they will feel more positive about themselves and school. So often, having the right attitude is half the battle.

In Chapter 5 we discussed the career counseling function, the importance of its mission, and the monumental role it plays in helping change the paradigm of the schooling process. In Figure 5.1, we listed seven roles for the counselor. Following is a list of more comprehensive steps, strategies, and roles for career guidance and counseling personnel.

Steps, Strategies, and Roles for Career Guidance and Counseling Personnel

1. *Become a believer and champion for work-based learning and school-to-work transition programs for all students.* Counselors who have been more oriented toward counseling the college bound need to consider a wider range of careers for their students. Counselors, like teachers, can participate in all kinds of professional development activities that emphasize school-to-work programs and can visit modern industries. They must accept that only 20–25% of the work force needs a bachelor's degree.

2. *Initiate Individual Career Development Plans (ICDPs).* Counseling and guidance personnel at all levels can play a major role in initiating ICDPs. They can also work with teachers on using ICDPs in the classroom. Review Chapter 5 for the 16 steps of the ICDP.

3. *Facilitate career majors and career cluster pathways for all students including the college bound.* Counselors can emphasize the importance of all students having a career major as well as influence the school in developing career cluster pathways that include the students pursuing university-driven careers. Counselors can work with teams of teachers to ensure broad career clusters.

4. *Influence the termination of the dual tracking of "career bound" and "college bound."* If we were to emphasize one major paradigm shift it would be to terminate the dual tracking of the college bound and the noncollege bound. No educator has the wisdom to really determine who is or is not capable of completing a college education. Counselors should not err by tracking any students away from lifelong learning.

5. *Educate parent groups regarding career options.* Our parent groups must be apprised of reform. Counselors can be instrumental in providing career information to parents and letting them know of the many great career opportunities that do not require a four-year degree.

6. *Influence faculty regarding work-based learning.* Because many teachers are content and discipline oriented, counselors can play a major role in selling work-based learning. They can work especially with faculty resistant to change by providing the latest information regarding school-to-work opportunities.

7. *Support articulated career paths.* One of the major changes proposed in school-to-work programs is articulated career paths that span elementary, secondary, community college, and university levels. Counselors are in a good position to work with faculty and administrators to encourage articulated career path programs. Current examples of this include counselors working with the

Tech Prep consortia that include secondary schools, community colleges, and universities with 2 + 2 + 2 articulated programs (2 years high school, 2 years community college, and 2 years university) for various careers.

8. ***Build connections between school and business industry groups.*** Unlike teachers, counselors have opportunities to schedule time with business and industry representatives and become instrumental in developing the necessary connections. We encourage counselors to play major roles in school, business, and industry partnership committees. As with the suggestions for teachers, the Chamber of Commerce and small business organizations will be instrumental in providing initial contacts with interested businesses.

9. ***Provide comprehensive information on all career options without bias.*** Most counselors have traditionally worked more with college-bound students than noncollege-bound students. We believe that because counselors themselves are products of the university, they are more acquainted with the university route and tend to be less knowledgeable about non-university-driven careers. Counselors must realize that 80% of careers do not require bachelor's degrees and be nonbiased when providing career counseling.

10. ***Develop public relations materials in support of school-to-work concepts.*** As we discussed earlier, all the public relations that can be mustered will be needed to reform education from content-based learning to work-based learning. Counselors will play a major role in promoting work-based learning and school-to-work concepts through the various methods listed in the suggestions for classroom teachers.

Administrators

We have not specifically discussed the role of administrators in work-based learning and school-to-work transition. Much of the prior discussion throughout the book, however, relates to administration. Administrators at all levels of education play a major role in the schooling process. It is well accepted that administrators set the tone and are the catalyst and coaches for change (Figure 10.1). The administration can dictate stagnation and business as usual or foster and nurture openness and change. The new mode of administration and manage-

Figure 10.1
Three C's for
Administration

Three C's for Administration

C
atalytic

oaches for

hange

ment in business and industry is to empower workers to do their jobs. It is time for educational institutions to adopt such administrative and organizational philosophies and empower teachers and counselors to do their jobs.

Steps, Strategies, and Roles for Administration

1. *Become a believer and champion for work-based learning and school-to-work transition programs for all students.* It is imperative that administrators, like counselors and teachers, be champions of work-based learning and school-to-work opportunities for all students. Administrators, because they set the climate for the school and hold financial control, are a great influence on educational reform.

2. *Establish an open climate that nurtures change.* Administrators may provide an open climate conducive to experimentation and change or perpetuate a closed controlling climate that stymies creativity, growth, and change. The iron-fisted controlling administrator is an antiquated model.

3. *Nurture creativity and experimentation of new strategies and methods.* Creative innovation is needed in the early stages of reform. The new school leader will nurture and encourage such creativity and change.

4. *Provide leadership support for dynamic professional development activities, for example, funding support and release time.* As we discussed in Chapter 9, the master key for work-based learning is professional development. Every professional development strategy possible should be implemented to help reform education. Administrators hold the key to providing release time and in-service policies required for effective professional development.

5. *Participate in professional development activities.* Administrators must be role models and participate in all possible professional development. Administrators are the leaders.

6. *Initiate and develop partnerships with business, industry, government, and labor.* Because administrators are the school leaders, they have the opportunities to meet with business and industry, government, and labor groups. They can develop the necessary partnerships that support work-based learning and school-to-work programs.

7. *Develop relationships and articulation agreements with other educational agencies.* Articulation, both horizontal and vertical, is desirable as we develop career pathways for learning. Administrators have a major responsibility to lead and approve such articulation between educational institutions and agencies.

8. *Provide an environment that encourages educational practitioners (classroom teachers) to perform at their most effective levels.* We believe administrators must nurture the best performance of all employed in the school setting. This can only be done by being supportive and setting a positive atmosphere that draws out the best from each member of the team.

9. *Support and encourage innovative restructuring, for example, block scheduling and alternating schedules.* Since innovative restructuring is required

for work-based learning and school-to-work initiatives to be effective, administrators must encourage, support, and assist in every way possible to establish new methods of doing business.

10. *Organize school-based and job-based work-based learning strategies.* Work-based learning strategies require innovative organizing and scheduling. Administrators need to strongly support both school-based and job-based strategies in order for *all* students to have such experiences.

11. *Be instrumental in educating parents and community groups about the new schooling process.* One of the major jobs of all school leaders is to be instrumental in working with parent and community groups. Public relations is needed and administration should be the primary leader.

12. *Be a catalytic coach for change.* Remember, if you are not part of the solution, you are part of the problem.

Business and Industry Personnel

Chapter 8 discussed the roles that business and industry can play in reinventing the schooling process. In developing positive linkages and connections between school and work, business and industry involvement will be critical.

Steps, Strategies, and Roles for Business and Industry Personnel

1. *Become a believer in and champion for work-based learning and school-to-work transition programs for all students.* Local business and industry leaders must recognize that they too should champion the cause of work-based learning and school-to-work transition by playing active roles in the education and preparation of our youth.

2. *Serve on school/industry committees, for example, advisory and partnership arrangements.* To prepare our young people for their roles in our work-oriented society, business and industry personnel must participate in various school/industry committees such as curriculum and advisory committees.

3. *Serve on local planning and steering committees.* We encourage the establishment of school-to-work steering committees at every school site. Business and industry representatives should be on such committees and play an active role.

4. *Participate in curriculum development.* The new career learning pathways require new curriculum with active connections to the real world. Business and industry representation is imperative in developing the new curriculum.

5. *Develop and provide mentorships.* Mentorships for students require that business/industry personnel be willing to serve in such capacities and assist young people in learning about various career options.

6. *Provide business and industry tours for students and faculty.* One of the more meaningful ways for students and faculty to become aware of the new

American work force is for tours to be provided in a variety of business and industry establishments.

7. *Participate in school/industry speaker bureaus.* The new connections require industries to be brought into the classroom in every way possible. One way to do so is to have business and industry speakers available to the schools.

8. *Participate in apprentice and internship programs.* In order to provide hands-on experiences, industry people must be willing to provide internship and apprentice programs in careers where such experiences are appropriate.

9. *Provide co-op training sites.* Co-op education requires business and industry participation in providing the training sites.

10. *Provide summer internships.* As work-based learning expands, summer internships will become a meaningful strategy. Internships in industry allow students to get extensive experience in a job setting that can greatly add relevancy to their school-based program.

11. *Participate in job shadowing.* For younger students, one of the better ways to become aware of various careers is to participate in job shadowing. Business and industry personnel play the major role in providing such experiences.

12. *Sponsor awards, grants, and scholarships.* One of the more meaningful ways for business and industry to participate in the schooling process is by sponsoring various awards and scholarships that highlight excellence in occupational program achievement. Many industries provide scholarships to technical and community colleges for study in certain career areas.

13. *Assist in setting career standards.* As work-based learning and school-to-work transition receive greater attention, one of the major concerns will be to set career standards and levels of achievement necessary for various careers. The development of such standards will depend greatly on business/industry input.

14. *Cooperate in facility and equipment sharing.* With the rapid technological development projected, new and different methods for providing students with the experiences desired in various career pursuits will be necessary. Innovative strategies of cooperation and sharing of facilitates and equipment will be necessary.

15. *Provide internships for educators.* In addition to providing internships for students, business and industry will also need to provide internship experiences for teachers, counselors, and administrators in environments in which their students will need to be successful.

16. *Provide mentors to teachers.* Industries can play a very meaningful role by providing mentors for teachers to build better connections between school and work.

17. *Assist with professional development.* As mentioned earlier, professional development is a major key to implementing work-based learning and school-to-work experiences. Business and industry can play a meaningful role in the professional development needed by all educators to form the connections between school and work (see Chapter 9 for a list of several strategies).

18. *Form partnerships with schools, for example, adopt-a-school programs,*

joint research, and experimentation projects. The type of partnerships that can be formed are endless. They can range from the more formal such as adopt-a-school program to simply telephoning a local school to find out how a business representative can participate in the educational system.

19. ***Participate in public relations programs and activities.*** Public relations is simply a useful method for educating citizens and other industry representatives. A good idea that few know about is not worth much.

20. ***Participate in career fairs for schools.*** The end result for students is rewarding opportunities. By participating in career fairs, students can be exposed to opportunities.

21. ***Publicize school/work connections.*** By helping get the word out, the school-to-work movement can gather momentum at a quicker rate. Note that number 20 emphasizes school programs and activities; this step publicizes the concept of school/work connections.

Summary

The lists in this chapter should stimulate ideas and help you implement work-based learning and school-to-work transition programs. Again, the lists are not intended to be inclusive; their purpose is to jog your mind and guide you in developing the new schooling process. As school-to-work transition programs grow, other innovative steps, strategies, and roles will evolve.

Change requires looking at things differently. Einstein is credited for having once said, "Significant problems cannot be solved at the same level of thinking with which we created them." We must move, therefore, to a new level of thinking about the purpose and role of our educational system.

One criticism of educational reform often discussed is that it remains too long at the talking stage before moving to action. Change is not easy and the task at hand is monumental; however, change and reform have been discussed for a long time. We, as a society, need to stop discussing change and start changing. Certainly many new ideas are being realized. Tech Prep, for example, has been implemented throughout practically every state and good results are reported. However, in many places there is more talk than action. One of our favorite statements often used by Dale Parnell summarizes the current stage of educational reform quite well: "Since everyone knows the problem, we need to adopt the Noah principle: No more prizes for predicting rain, prizes *only* for building arks."

 It is now time to build. The rewards are for the students, educators, and communities building positive connections between schooling and living successful, productive lives.

Chapter **11**

Closing Thoughts

"The key to both productivity and competitiveness is the skill of our people and our capacity to use highly educated and trained people to maximum advantage in the workforce . . . the guiding principle on which our educational and industrial systems have been built is profoundly different; this guiding principle, for long highly successful, is now outmoded and harmful, and the time has come to change it."
(Marshall & Tucker, 1992)

When we began this book, there was one main point we wanted to emphasize: We need an educational system that incorporates *from the beginning, a theme or focus that people work to live and that there is a positive connectedness between the schooling process and living productive lives.* As Marshall and Tucker indicate, the guiding principle of the past system is outmoded. It is time to get rid of the antiquated, content-based, classicist schooling process that is unconnected to the real world. The underlying basic foundation and basic philosophical paradigm for our educational system must now be changed. Our focus has been on the philosophical changes needed, many of which are radical compared to the current educational system. The concepts and implementation strategies we presented are approaches to achieving the new paradigm.

We are somewhat perplexed by the continuing complacency and resistance among educators to change, especially since there is a growing dissatisfaction in the educational system throughout society at large. Most educators still do not accept the basic premise of a positive connectedness between schooling and the real world. Business and industry management styles switched a number of years ago from a closed to open system perspective. A closed system perspective focuses on the internal environment without considering any external environmental factors. Today's managers in modern industry realize they must manage using an open system philosophy if they want to survive. Why do most educators feel they can continue to operate our educational system unconnected to the real world? Because of the technological changes and the changing educational needs of society, education must now be managed with an open system mentality. This implies listening to your customers (students and the community at large) and adapting to social, political, legal, demographic, technological, and economic conditions. The result of this mentality will be greater interaction with society and extensive partnerships with business and industry.

When it comes to change, educators seem to be more reactive than proactive. Our educational system appears to be slow in reacting to global and technological changes. Perhaps the problems are not significant enough for educators to be concerned. U.S. industries that were threatened by foreign competition did not react until they began to lose business. There is something about human nature that requires hitting rock bottom before change can occur. We ask: When will we believe education has hit rock bottom? Unmotivated students, unqualified graduates for job openings, and high dropout rates are apparently not enough. There is no question that educators are concerned about these problems, but apparently not enough to be willing to change. The escalation in discussion about voucher systems and privatization of schools, for example, is probably a direct reaction to public dissatisfaction with the educational system. The implementation of these ideas may be the mechanisms that pressure educators to change. Competition has a way of making people adapt or else become obsolete.

If we wait until the vast global and technical changes are in full force, we will be lagging behind. With production facilities, money, and technology crossing international boundaries with ease, developed countries will retain their competitiveness only through people. It is well established that the key to remaining globally competitive is by developing a highly skilled and educated work force. The importance of maintaining a competitive edge is not to be underestimated; once such an advantage erodes far enough, it is very difficult to regain.

This book has been primarily about making major philosophical and systemic changes in the paradigm of education in this country. If the philosophical mindset changes are made, no doubt the appropriate strategies and techniques will follow. Based on our research, study and observations, as well as the School-To-Work Opportunities Act of 1994 we believe there are several significant ingredients that must be incorporated into our educational system. We therefore strongly recommend the following 15 ingredients to be included in the New Educational Paradigm.

- The central mission of education is to prepare everyone for *further learning* and *productive employment*.
- All education is success oriented.
- The schooling process no longer sorts students on the basis of academic ability.
- Tracking is by career interests and abilities instead of academic abilities.
- All young people must have a career major.
- All students must be in a career cluster pathway of learning that leads to achieving their career major.
- University-driven careers are within career clusters along with related non-university-driven careers.

- Career counseling is an integral part of the schooling process that starts at the elementary level.
- All students must have an Individual Career Development Plan that guides them through their career development process.
- The career cluster pathways are articulated, seamless paths of learning that span elementary, secondary, postsecondary, community college, and university levels according to the career major.
- Academic and occupational preparation are integrated in the career cluster pathways.
- All learning is taught in an applied, contextual, relevant manner.
- Assessment is couched in diagnostic performance.
- Work-based learning—both school-based and job-based experiences—are integral parts of the schooling process for all students.
- Business and industry are partners in the educational process for preparing our youth to live successful lives.

The changes we are endorsing are no less than monumental. Although much of what we have recommended is idealistic, it is, however, quite logical considering the needs of society as we approach the twenty-first century. Many question whether such a significant paradigm shift is possible. While the change we are proposing is overwhelming, there have been bigger challenges in this world that have been overcome. There are many examples of businesses, industries, and even countries that have completely altered their systems. One of the biggest turnarounds has occurred in Japan, once synonymous with poor quality, now highly respected for excellent standards of manufacturing.

In agreement with the editors of *Education Week* and other authors, we believe there is a growing recognition of the mis-match between the worlds inside and outside of school which is launching a quest for a new model of schools—a New Paradigm. We therefore challenge you, the reader, with the concepts discussed in this book; we encourage you to rethink the current educational practices and processes. Is this book going to be read and forgotten? Or will you use it to seriously think about the purpose of the schooling process in the United States? Ponder and discuss what has been written. We challenge *you* to go beyond and take positive *action*.

So we have come full circle . . .
  Societies maintaining educational systems that nurture knowledge acquisition at the exclusion of knowledge application will soon find both their ideologies and technologies eroding.

References

Editors of *Education Week* (1993). *From Risk to Renewal: Charting the Course for Reform.* Washington, DC: Education Week.

Marshall, R., & Tucker, M. (1992). *Thinking for a Living.* New York: Basic, p. xvi.

Selected Readings and Bibliography

Academy for Educational Development. (1989). *Partnership for Learning: School Completion and Employment Preparation in the High School Academies*. New York: Author.

Bailey, T. (1994). *Barriers to Employer Participation in School-to-Work Transition Programs*. Paper prepared for a seminar on Employer Participation in School-to-Work Transition Programs, the Brookings Institution, Washington, DC.

Bailey, T., & Merritt, D. (1992, May). *School-to-Work Transition and Youth Apprenticeship in the United States* Working paper prepared for Manpower Research Demonstration Corporation.

Berryman, S. E., & Bailey, T. (1992). *The Double Helix of Education and the Economy*. New York: Institute on Education and the Economy, Columbia University.

Boyer, E. L. (1992, November). "Curriculum, Culture and Social Cohesion." *Leadership Abstracts* 5(2). League for Innovation in the Community College. Laguna, CA.

Brustein, M., & Mahler, M. (1994). *AVA Guide to the School-to-Work Opportunities Act*. Alexandria, VA: American Vocational Association.

Caine, R., & Caine, G. (1991). *Making Connections: Teaching and the Human Brain*. Alexandria, VA: Association for Supervision and Curriculum Development.

Carnevale, A. P. (1991). *America and the New Economy*. A report prepared for the U.S. Department of Labor. Washington, DC: U.S. Government Printing Office.

Cheek, G. D., & Campbell, C. P. (1994). "School-to-Work Lessons from Abroad." *Tech Directions* 53(7), pp. 11–21.

Clinchy, E. (1994, June). "Higher Education: The Albatross Around the Neck of Our Public Schools." *Phi Delta Kappan* 75(10), pp. 745–751.

Commission on the Skills of the American Workforce. (1990). *America's Choice: High Skills or Low Wages*. Rochester, NY: National Center on Education and the Economy.

Council of Chief State School Officers. (1992). *Connecting School and Employment: Policy Statement 1991*. Washington, DC: Author.

Dornsife, C. (1991). *Beyond Articulation: The Department of Tech Prep Programs*. A monograph prepared for the National Center for Research in Vocational Education. Berkeley: University of California.

Editors of *Education Week* (1993). *From Risk to Renewal: Charting the Course for Reform*. Washington, DC: *Education Week*.

Fiske, E. B. (1991). *Smart Schools, Smart Kids*. New York: Simon & Schuster.

Gardner, H. (1983). *Frames of Mind: The Theory of Multiple Intelligences*. New York: Basic.

Goodlad, J. (1984). *A Place Called School*. New York: McGraw-Hill.

Grubb, W. N. (1989). *Separating the Wheat from the Chaff: The Role of Vocational Education in Economic Development*. Berkeley, CA: National Center for Research in Vocational Education.

Grubb, W. N., Davis, D., Lum, J., Plihal, J., & Morgaine, C. (1990). *The Cunning Hand, The Cultured Mind: Models for Integrating Vocational and Academic Education*. Berkeley, CA: National Center for Research in Vocational Education.

Hamilton, S. F. (1990). *Apprenticeship for Adulthood: Preparing Youth for the Future*. New York: Free Press.

Hoerner, J. L. (1991–92). "Breaking the Mold: Tech Prep and the New Paradigm." *ATEA Journal 20*(2), pp. 11–15.

Hoerner, J. L. (1994, February–March). "Work-Based Learning: The Key to School-to-Work Transition." *ATEA Journal 21*(3), pp. 6–10.

Hull, D. (1993). *Opening Minds, Opening Doors: The Rebirth of American Education*. Waco, TX: Center for Occupational Research and Development.

Hull, D., & Parnell, D. (1991). *Tech Prep/Associate Degree: A Win/Win Experience*. Waco, TX: Center for Occupational Research and Development.

Imel, S. (1993). *Youth Apprenticeship: Trends and Issues Alerts* (ED 359 375). Washington, DC: Office of Educational Research and Improvement.

Ingles, P. (1994). "Electric Avenue: A Utility Company's Work Experience Program Broadens Opportunities for Students." *American Vocational Journal 69*(5), pp. 28–30.

Jacobs, H. (Eds.). (1989). *Interdisciplinary Curriculum: Design and Implementation*. Alexandria, VA: Association for Supervision and Curriculum.

Jacobs, R. L. (1990). *Structured On-the-Job Training. Training and Development Research Report* (ED 326 641). Columbus, Ohio: The Ohio State University.

Kappner, A. (1993, January). A speech given at the League for Innovation in the Community College. *Workforce 2000 Conference*, New Orleans, LA.

Kolb, D. A. (1984). *Experiential Learning: Experience as the Source of Learning and Development*. Englewood Cliffs, NJ: Prentice-Hall.

Jobs for the Future. (1991). *Essential Elements of Youth Apprenticeship Programs: A Preliminary Outline*. Cambridge, MA: Author.

Johnson, W. B., & Packer, A. E. (1987). *Workforce 2000*. Indianapolis: Hudson Institute.

Lester, J. N. (1994, January). *U.S. Adults Say High Schools Are Not Doing Enough to Help Students Develop Job Skills, Find Jobs and Plan Careers, Says New Gallup Survey*. A paper and presentation given at the National Press Club, Washington, DC.

Marshall, R., & Tucker, M. (1992). *Thinking for a Living: Work, Skills, and the Future of the American Economy*. New York: Basic.

McLaughlin, A., Bennett, W. B., & Verity, C. W. (1988, July). *Building a Quality Workforce*. Washington, DC: U.S. Department of Labor.

Muffo, J. (1994, May). *Jobs, Jobs, Jobs, Quality Improvement in Action*. Academic Assessment Program. Blacksburg, VA: Virginia Polytechnic Institute and State University.

National Alliance of Business. (1991). *The Compact Project: Final Report*. Washington, DC: Author.

National Coalition for Advanced Manufacturing. (1993). *Preparing Technical Workers for the New Industrial Era: The Need for a Fundamental Shift in Federal Policy Toward*

Technical Education. A Position Paper. National Coalition for Advanced Manufacturing, Washington, DC.

National Commission on Excellence in Education. (1983). *A Nation at Risk: The Imperative for Educational Reform.* Washington, DC: Author.

National Youth Employment Coalition and William T. Grant Foundation Commission on Work, Family and Citizenship—Youth and America's Future. (1992, December). *Making Sense of Federal Job Training Policy: 24 Expert Recommendations to Create "A Comprehensive and Unified Federal Job Training System."* Washington, DC: National Youth Employment Coalition and The William T. Grant Foundation Commission.

103rd Congress. (1994, March). Goals 2000: Educate America Act, H.R. 1804.

103rd Congress. (1994, May). School-to-Work Opportunities Act of 1994 H.R. 2884.

Orr, M. (1993). "Urban Regimes and School Compacts: The Development of the Detroit Compact." *Urban Review* 25(2), pp. 105–120.

Osterman, P. (1980). *Getting Started: The Youth Labor Market.* Cambridge, MA: MIT Press.

Osterman, P. (1994). *Strategies for Involving Employers in School-to-Work Programs.* Prepared for a conference at the Brookings Institution, Washington, DC.

Parnell, D. (1985). *The Neglected Majority.* Washington, DC: Community College Press.

Parnell, D. (1994). *LogoLearning: Searching for Meaning in Education.* Waco, TX: Center for Occupational Research and Development.

Pennington, H. (1992, October). *Youth Apprenticeship Program.* A presentation at the National Tech Prep Conference. Chicago, IL.

"Quid Pro Quo." (1994). *Vocational Education Journal* 69(5), pp. 22–23, 39.

Reich, R. (1992). *The Work of Nations.* New York: Vintage.

Reich, R., & Riley, R. (1993, September). *Breaking the Mold.* Berkeley, CA: National Center for Research in Vocational Education Teleconference.

Rigden, D. W. (1991). *Business/School Partnerships: A Path to Effective School Restructuring.* New York: Council for Aid to Education.

Secretary's Commission on Achieving Necessary Skills. (1991, June). *What Work Requires of Schools: A SCANS Report for America 2000.* Washington, DC: U.S. Department of Labor.

Secretary's Commission on Achieving Necessary Skills. (1992). *Learning a Living: A Blueprint for High Performance.* Washington, DC: U.S. Government Printing Office.

Shanker, A. (1988, June 26). ". . . And the School-Student Connection." *New York Times,* p. E7.

Shlaes, A. (1994, April 26). "Re-employment That Kills Jobs." *Wall Street Journal,* p. A22.

Simon, R. I., Dippo, D., & Schenko, A. (1991). *Learning Work: A Critical Pedagogy of Work Education.* New York: Bergin & Garvey.

Smith, C. L., & Rojewski, J. W. (1992). *School-to-Work: Alternatives for Educational Reform* (ED 354 303).

Stern, D. (1991, March). *Combining School and Work: Options in High Schools and Two-Year Colleges.* Washington, DC: Office of Vocational and Adult Education, U.S. Department of Education.

Stern, D., Raby, M., & Dayton, C. (1992). *Career Academies: Partnerships for Reconstructing American High Schools.* San Francisco, CA: Jossey-Bass.

Stern, D., Stone, J., III, Hopkins, D., McMillion, M., & Crain, R. (1994). *School-Based Enterprise: Productive Learning in American High Schools*. San Francisco, CA: Jossey-Bass.

Thurow, L. (1992). *Head to Head: The Coming Economic Battle Among Japan, Europe, and America*. New York: Morrow.

"U.S. Economy May Dominate for Years." (1994, January 10). *Wall Street Journal*, p. A1.

Vocational Education and Training in Europe: A Four-Country Study in Four Employment Sectors. (1992). London: Further Education Unit (ED 353 473).

Wessel, D., & Benjamin, D. (1994, March 14). "Looking for Work: In Employment Policy, America and Europe Make a Sharp Contrast." *Wall Street Journal*, pp. A1–A5.

Whitehead, A. (1929). *The Aims of Education and Other Essays*. New York: Macmillan.

William T. Grant Foundation Commission on Work, Family and Citizenship—Youth and America's Future. (1988, November). *The Forgotten Half: Non-College Youth in America*. Washington, DC: Author.

William T. Grant Foundation Commission on Work, Family and Citizenship—Youth and America's Future. (1992, December). *Youth Apprenticeship in America: Guidelines for Building an Effective System*. Washington, DC: Author.

Wirth, A. G. (1992). *Education and Work for the Year 2000: Choices We Face*. San Francisco, CA: Jossey-Bass.

Index

Academies, career, 11, 29, 30–31
Act, 9, 41–42
Administrators, 22–23, 114–116
Apprentice programs, 11, 29, 34–36, 88
Assessment, student, 72–77
Attendance, students on job, 94

Barriers to work-based learning, 94–95
Boeing Company, 86, 96
Business/education partnerships, 11, 29,
    40–41, 83–97, 111–113, 116–117

Career academies, 11, 29, 30–31
Career clusters, 42, 60, 111, 113
Career counseling, 45–53
Career development, 49–52
Career development continuum, 62
Career major, 54–64
Career paths, 12–14, 29, 111, 113
Certification, teacher, 105
Change, potential for, 21–23
Class projects, 34
Clinical experiences, 11, 20, 37
College completion rate, 1
College-bound students, 23, 71, 77–78
College needs assessment survey, 18, 46
Community relations, 112
Community service learning, 11, 29, 40
Competencies, 72

Contextual learning theory, 23–25, 71–72
Cooperative education, 11, 29, 36–37
Cost-benefit analysis, 90–94
Council of Chief State School Officers
    (CCSSO), 6, 46
Counseling, 45–53, 112–114
Counselor, 52
Curriculum development, 65–82, 85
Curriculum integration models, 69
Customer service labs, 11, 29, 31–32

DACUM. *See also* Curriculum develop-
    ment
DACUM, 80–81
    definition, 87
Detroit, business/education partnership
    in, 41, 93
Discipline, student, 94
Discipline, subject, 57–58, 66
Donations, 85
Downsizing, 94–95
Dualism, 5, 22–23, 60–61

Educational system, critique of, 1–8,
    16–27
Elementary school teachers, training,
    105–106
Employees, needed characteristics of,
    18–19

Enterprises, school-based, 11, 29
Equipment, 85
Experiential learning, 24–25

Gallup survey of career counseling, 47
Germany, employment training in, 87–90
Goals 2000: Educate America Act, 6
Grant, William T., Foundation, 38
Great American Academic and Social
    Sorting System, defined, 21
Guidance staff. *See* Counseling

Human resource development, 22–23

ICDP. *See* Individual Career Develop-
    ment Plan
In-service training, 84, 104–105
Individual Career Development Plan
    (ICDP), 4, 49–52, 112, 113
Industry. *See* Business/education partner-
    ship
Integrated day curriculum, 67, 69
Interdisciplinary units/courses, 67
Internship, 11, 29, 39

Japan, employment training in, 87–90
Job shop labs, 11, 29, 32
Job simulation labs, 11, 29, 32–33
Job-based learning, 11, 29, 34–43, 84, 86.
    See also Work-based learning

Labs, 11, 29, 31–33
Loyalty, building employee, 91–92

Masters. *See also* Apprentice programs
Masters, 86–87
Mathematics, 20–21
Medical model, 77
Mentors, 11, 29, 38–39, 86–87
Milwaukee, business/industry partnership
    in, 109

National Coalition for Advanced Manu-
    facturing, 3
National Commission on Excellence in
    Education, 16
National Tooling and Machining Associ-
    ation, 93

On-the-job training (OJT), 11, 29, 37–38

Parallel disciplines, curriculum and,
    66–67
Parents, involving, 112, 113
Perkins, Carl D., Vocational and Applied
    Technology Education Peu Higher
    Education Roundtable, 18
Philosophy, educational, 16–27
Plato, 19
Postsecondary schools, 70–71
PreService education, 102–104
Professional development, 98–107
Public relations, 112, 114
    requirements of, 10

Responsibility, teaching, 57–58

SCANS (Secretary's Commission on
    Achieving Necessary Skills),
    72–75
School-based enterprises, 11, 29
Scheduling, 111
School-to-Work Opportunities Act of
    1994
    background on, 17, 43
    business role in, 85–86, 111–112
    career guidance and, 47–48, 59–60
    curriculum guide, 65–66, 70
    general program requirements of, 10
    skill certificate definition, 87
Schools, summer jobs and, 11, 29
Schools. *See also* Curriculum develop-
    ment; Teachers; awareness in,
    100–102
    businesses and, 84–86
    integrating work learning in, 70
    summer jobs and, 11, 29
    work experience in, 11, 29, 29–34

Secretary's Commission on Achieving
    Necessary Skills. *See* SCANS
Senior projects, 34
Site-based learning. *See* Work-based
    learning
Skill certificate, defined, 87
Southern California Edison Company, 86
Speakers, 85
Strategies, 28–44
Students. *See also* Counseling
    assessment of, 72–77
    job attendance problems, 94
Summer school for teachers, 106
Summer jobs, 40
Supplies, 85

Tax incentives, 95
Taylor model, 55–56
Teacher certification, 105
Teacher colleges, 102–104
    awareness needed in, 100–102
    elementary school, 105–106

in-service education, 84–85
preservice education, 98–107
work-based learning plan, 108–112
Tech Prep Education Act, 9, 41–43
Testing, 74–77
Tours, of businesses and industries, 85
Tracking, educational, 50, 71, 113
Transition steering committee, 112

Vocational/occupational labs, 11, 29, 33

WIN model. *See* Work incentive model
Work-based learning plan
    integration of, 70
    plan, three-part foundation, 74
    changing needs of, 54–56
    learning plan, definition, 2–15
    learning plan, implementation of,
        108–118
    learning plan, seven-step model,
        100–102
Work-study, 11, 29, 39